I0012498

CHIPPING-AWAY AT BUREAUCRATIC OBSTRUCTION

The opposing productivities of IT and chips

Author

Dr Maurice J Perks

This book is dedicated to my late wife, Cynthia, and my wife, Penny.

It is also a means of thanking anyone who taught me facts and knowledge. Most of all encouraged me to think. Especially to think out-of-the-box differently, realising where the sides of the box are.

Sometimes this has been by direct teaching and lecturing. Sometimes this has been indirectly by the examples they have set that I have been privileged to follow. People with whom I have worked and admired. People who inspired and, in some cases, still inspire me … **Thanks.**

Below are some words penned by my good friend John Whitney CBE who was Chairman of the Royal Academy of Drama RADA (2003 – 2007)

> *Jealousy cannot be witnessed. Cannot be seen.*
> *Cannot be touched, Is invisible.*
> *Has no principles. Turns love to hatred.*
> *Never departs. Never concedes.*
> *Is always watchful. Seeks no remedy.*
> *Plays the part. Gives the quarter.*
> *Needs no investment. Is unforgiving.*
> *Is alert to weakness and is fearless to the grave.*

I was, and still am, moved by those words, and in writing this book, I suddenly realised that you could apply them in many ways if you replace the subject word *Jealousy* with other words. So, for this book, I have replaced the word *Jealousy* with the term **Obstructive Bureaucracy**. This term is explained as the book proceeds, but for the moment, it should be self-explanatory. So, this is the result of my modifications to John's original.

> **Obstructive Bureaucracy** *cannot be directly witnessed. Cannot be directly seen.*
> *Cannot be touched, Is invisible.*
> *Has no principles. Turns the love of something to hatred.*
> *Never departs. Never concedes.*
> *Is always watchful. Seeks no remedy.*
> *Plays the part. Gives no quarter.*
> *Needs no direct investment. Is unforgiving.*
> *Is alert to weakness and is fearless to the grave.*

This book aims to reduce the effects of **Obstructive Bureaucracy** and banish it to the other side of the Universe, wherever that is.

author is not responsible for errors, inaccuracies and any ommissions that change the contents.

This copy is Version 1.1 of the book.

1. Contents

2. Foreword

The enemy amongst us

I've written this book because, throughout my life, my mind has grated and rebelled when I have come upon what we generally term *bureaucracy*. I intensely dislike bureaucracy, and my observations are that I am not alone.

I'm not going to define bureaucracy here and now; that is something that this book does as it flows. But I will say that bureaucracy is one of those challenges that when we encounter it in one of its many forms, we recognise it. It's different for different people, but in general, it's frustrating. Most of us have the impression that it's increasing and that we see it as unfavourable for our happiness and wellbeing, not to mention our finances. What's happening is the subject and concern of this book. Where's it coming from and why? Here's an opinion which this book explores and tries to explain.

Put together these two statements:

1. Bureaucracy seems to be increasing as we proceed through our lives. Both our personal and work lives. Everywhere we bump into it, and it bumps into us. We feel claustrophobic about it. Somehow our freedoms are being penned-in and restricted.
2. Our society is increasingly being defined and redefined by our use of Information Technology (IT); consequently, digital bureaucracy is everywhere. So many of our interfaces in our daily routines are through digital devices.

As this book describes, bureaucracy today is often covert and hidden. As we have said, it seems to be increasing. We shall see that it is IT that is enabling it to grow. For me, as the author, bureaucracy can often be an enemy of progress. Progress to where is debatable, so read on.

Our challenge

The UK, an advanced industrial nation with arguably the fifth most prosperous global economy,[1] has what 'the experts'[2] consider to be low economic growth. Quarter after quarter, year after year, the growth rates experienced, pre the Covid-19 pandemic are deemed meagre by those who are 'in-the-know' and some who do know. To those of us 'not-in-the-know', they seem small.

---

[1] This is pre-COVID pandemic.
[2] Whoever they are and wherever they are?

Sometimes the growth rates are negative; we shrank. The economy around us shrank. Sometimes, as individuals, it seems that we shrank along with it and our personal-wealth decreased. We ask *why?* The answers are often complicated and hard to grasp.

The reason for the low-performance puzzles many of the most renowned experts, let alone the average citizen. The experts can't come to a single conclusion. Many books try to explain the drag and sag in the numerous graphs that chart the progress or lack of it. No successful solution to the challenge seems to have been identified yet alone proven. As a nation, especially a country within the continent of Europe, we are not alone with our tardy national growth. That is cold comfort. Whether in or out of the European Community (EC), we are not sole and unique. It's a matter of national culture, which is hard to analyse and even harder to define with certainty.

Recent examples of UK economic growth

This table below shows the recent UK economic growth rates by quarter. The source is Trading Economics[3]. They are before the dramatic effects of the Covid-19 pandemic, which is considered elsewhere in this book.

Year by Quarter	% UK Economic Growth by Quarter	Global Economic Growth by Year
1Q 2017	0.6	3.1
2Q	0.3	
3Q	0.3	
4Q	0.4	
1Q 2018	0.1	3.6
2Q	0.5	
3Q	0.6	
4Q	0.2	
1Q 2019	0.6	3.2
2Q	-0.1	
3Q	0.5	
4Q	0.0	
1Q 2020	-3.0	-4.8 (1Q)
2Q	?	

Figure 1 Recent Economic Growth

---

[3] https://tradingeconomics.com/united-kingdom/gdp-growth

The figures quoted above are illustrative, and there may be more precise figures available.

When writing this book, the Coronavirus epidemic, which is transforming into a pandemic, is threatening to make the UK's growth and global economic growth highly damaging. This may be so, and the forecasters will get the numbers wrong with their customary and consistent inaccuracy. Others will heap blame on the pandemic as the root cause of the negative growth. But the age-old underlying cause will still exist. Part of this cause will, as the book proceeds, be suggested and hopefully explained.

Recent statements on Economic Growth

After lunch, on the 11th March 2020 in The Houses of Parliament, Westminster, London, UK, the Chancellor of the Exchequer the Rt. Honourable Rishi Sunak delivered his first budget to the Parliament and thereby to the British nation. In it, he said that the Office of Budgetary Responsibility (OBR)[4] was downgrading UK economic growth for 2020 to 1.1% (average about 0.3% per quarter) from the Spring 2019 forecast for 2020 of 1.4%. The downgrade made what was already a meagre number look more-meagre.

In February of 2021, The UK's Office of National Statistics reported that the UK economy in 2020 fell by 9.9%. This decline was twice the largest previous largest decline. Covid-19 and the lockdown strategy to contain its spread was clearly the underlying cause. But the small numbers game returned. In December of 2020, the economy grew by 1.2% after a decline of 3.2% in November 2020.

Other sources suggested that in 2020, world economic growth might not be the 2.9% forecast in late 2019 but 2.4%. The main reason being the global affliction of the Coronavirus pandemic.

The blame game

Who is to blame is the daily question? Politicians blame other politicians past, present and sometimes those who haven't voted into any political office. Economists blame the economy because it never seems to match their forecasts. These forecasts are always correct when made based on the past and projections of what has happened. The underlying assumption seems to be that

Figure 2 What goes round comes round

---

[4] The OBR is a UK governmental function that is required to produce two economic forecasts per financial year.

everything in the future is the product of history. Under scrutiny, this would appear to rule out progress since nothing new and novel will ever happen?

Bankers blame factors outside their control like financial crises, which are not caused by what they say are their risk-averse activities. Many of which make gambling seem failsafe to the average person. Business management blames workers. Workers blame lousy management and politicians. Everyone blames taxation and underinvestment. Many blame the weather. COVID is a new source of blame, especially as it isn't of the human form and seems to have originated in The East.

The accusing fingers or the accusing cursors are pointed everywhere in this IT age, and the cycle continues. What goes around is round.

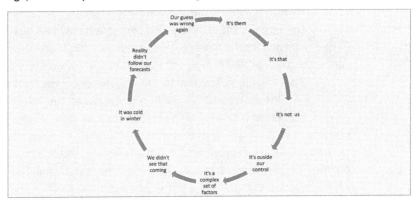

Figure 3 The wheel of fortune or lack of it.

The positives

A country like the UK has many factors that point to a positive environment. These should enable better economic growth, more remarkable than, let us say, a meagre one or two per cent. On its face, the outlook and the horizon seem positive, and substantial growth prospects are warm. The sunlit uppers beckon.

*Figure 4
Eureka*

Overall the UK population is by even any global standards educated and enlightened. This enlightenment is historical and is continually updated. Factors like the English language, which is the worldwide language of business and entertainment, are real. The UK has a robust educational system that supposedly hones abundant natural raw talent in many disciplines and has produced great minds and leaders for countless years. There is no reason to believe that this will not continue. Suddenly, the next Newton, Shakespeare, Faraday, or even The New Beatles will not appear.

There are an unmatched collection and tradition of stable technically-oriented institutions. Many of these, dating back to what is known as the steam-driven Industrial Revolution. The UK started and roared into action. But somehow, the dreary growth rates continue. The raw materials for the intellectual job seem to be there, but the product of profitable growth is not. Something is amiss. We are using something in the wrong way. This book points the finger of blame at IT and how embedded it is in business productivity and personal productivity.

We often hear that a lower starting point allows growth to appear proportional more significant than it is. This perception may well be correct. Even allowing for the mature state of the UK's public and private business sectors versus the levels at the end of the 20th century of the likes of India and China, it's hard to explain what we sometimes refer to as

Figure 5 A mind game?

The British Disease. We might rewrite that as The French Disease or The Italian Disease. This disease is not a medical condition; it is an economic condition, though the root cause may exist in our minds? Perhaps it may be somewhere in between. Or, is it as we shall discuss some cultural condition that afflicts us and many other nations. Is it a human characteristic held deep within our genes or a product of our history?

Once an organisation loses its spirit of pioneering and rests on its early work, its progress stops[5] – Thomas J Watson, founder of IBM (1874 to 1956)

We've got it taped

Many believe that the UK real entrepreneurial spirit is hindered by the dreaded and cumbersome spectre of what we refer to as Red Tape. Red tape has an image in the minds of many of us

of something bound by Red Tape, like a legal document. When you cut the tape, you become free from its constraints, and the world is your

Figure 7 No entry

Figure 6 This is a binding disagreement

oyster, so to speak. Red tape therefore binds, it constrains and restricts. It isn't pleasant. It is negative. It stops you from seeing

---

[5] It is up to the reader to decide whether this Thomas Watson quote is applicable to the aforementioned nation or the next mentioned union.

what is within that which is wrapped and thereby prevents you from benefitting from what is available as information within the bound document itself. It's a kind of censorship and shield. It constrains your knowledge, and knowledge is a part of progress.

Hope springs eternal and beyond

Hope, for the UK, is that much of this Red Tape will magically disappear with the long-awaited freedom from the European Union (EU). The direct links with Brussels, which may or may not be red, will be severed. This book claims that this is a long shot unless the fundamental underlying causes of Red Tape's strangleholds from all sources are recognised and irradicated. We now openly state that these causes have become fuelled by the very attitudes and technologies capable of producing growth rather than hindering it. It's a sort of shooting the national foot with technical lead shot[6].

Further, this book leads us to the proposition that we are replacing the physical Red Tape of yesteryear with today's Digital Red Tape. Digital Red Tape has happened with the advent of what we can call the Information Age or the Digital Age. Information Technology (IT) capabilities are being applied in a restraining way rather than an enabling way with the consequences of suppressed growth and opportunities missed. The potential of IT is misused for negative activities as well as positive activities.

There are two parts to this book.

This book is written in two parts:

Part 1 Obstructive Bureaucracy – the challenge of the chip and Digital Icebergs.

This first part covers the problems that we have with IT's application to produce economic growth and the interference of those who use it for harmful bureaucratic purposes. There is the consideration of historical bureaucracy, pointing out that there is nothing new about bureaucracy. Bureaucracy is as old as the hills and perhaps older.

Part 2 The Chipping-Away - solutions to Obstructive Bureaucracy

This part begins to define how we could better organise ourselves to minimise the disorganising influence of bureaucratic activities at governmental,

---

[6] It's interesting to note that the word lead rhymes with red.

business, and personal levels. The solution of how to banish **Obstructive Bureaucracy** to the far side of the Universe is not provided. A hint is proferred.

The COVID Factor

At last, we formally mention COVID-19 and the effects it has had on lifestyles in all parts of our world in 2020 and beyond. When the writing of this book started, COVID-19 was science-fiction. When its pandemic arrived, it did provide the author with plenty of spare time, through lockdown, to dash onwards with this book's contents. This time was an unexpected benefit.

As mentioned as the book proceeds, it also provided an unexpected opportunity for those who practice **Obstructive Bureaucracy** to execute their retarding art. As is so often the case in life, there are two sides to the coin. The good side of bureaucracy, which we discuss later, came into its own by organising matters that were, and still are, critical. The bad side got in the way as it usually does.

The effects of COVID-19 will be blamed for the lack of economic growth and progress in 2020 and many years after that. It is a factor, but the underlying factors that prevented profitable growth and progress before its appearance are still active unless de-activated.

Off we go then at last

At the start, this book mentions the progress that we humans are making. Progressing towards what we see and feel is *a smarter existence*. Then it discusses the history of the microchip. Please note that we have not yet defined what we mean by the chip. A definition will follow, but don't be surprised if we do not explain the chip in deeply technical electronic terms. It won't be like that. We shall discuss the usage of modern microchips and how their capabilities are employed in the Information Age. We shall explain and complain about how this usage achieves the aforementioned wounded national foot rather than the comfortable growth rates. Comfortable growth rates mean real economic progress instead of the near-stagnation of the national economy's meagre growth.

Somehow as a nation, and we are by no means alone. The UK has evolved a national characteristic that welcomes technology, especially welcoming Information Technology (IT). It uses IT in ways that can often be elite because the systems are only usable by an expert few. Or, it uses technology to self-defeat progress and

Figure 8 I don't do rush

efficiency in a covert manner. It's as though a car is driven with the throttle fully down and the brakes partially on. All seems well on the dashboard (digital, of course), but all is not well with the car's speed and efficiency on the road.

We are not alone

As we have already said, we here in the UK are indeed by no means alone with our national economic disease.

You are never alone with a clone.[7]

Anyone who has sought service or even a simple stamp in a French Post Office (La Poste) will have had ample time to observe the puzzling application of technology. Technology enables hopelessly bureaucratic processes to ensure that the queues remain long and strong. Thereby giving a clear sign of *la vie bureaucratique Français.* The author was once in a queue at a French Post Office. In the true spirit of Gallic Fraternity, he asked, in his unpolished French, an adjacent member of the line, what was going on? Why was the wait so long? The neighbouring queue brother replied with excellent English vocabulary and appropriate humour; *they are all making their wills and testaments.* I remember thinking, some won't do it in time. Luckily I got my stamp before lunchtime and enjoyed a three hour lunch hour in the best traditions of *la vie Francais.*

Don't expect this book to have a miracle answer to the challenges as pointed out so far. The book works by describing the key factors and characteristics that help explain the environment of business and any associated economics. It makes some statements about the root causes of the problems that beset profitable growth. This book is not filled with statistics but is wordy and descriptive to help anyone understand the challenges that we live with. It is not an academic and theoretical book. It is not a lesson in economics, not that there is a consistent one. It's merely a different and straightforward view with simple messages about how we are affected by bureaucracy. The word *bureaucracy* has been gently introduced into the text. It doesn't shock any potential reader and cause him or her to wrap up the book in red tape and propel it down a river out of frustration.

---

[7] It's not clear who first uttered this but we can hypothesise that it was more than one person.

Use carefully!

At the heart of these messages is the statement that we are misusing IT capabilities to slow down real growth. Sometimes we are misusing these capabilities to generate negative growth. We are using IT capabilities to generate Red Tape or call them; Red Systems with Digital Red Tape.

Bureaucracy Rules. OK? If you do or don't agree, fill in Form ZP143/04 – 12 in triplicate.

Who should read this book?

Anyone who hates bureaucracy and wants to understand how it affects our daily lives in this, the IT age, perhaps even wants to fight it. This book's contents are not highly technical nor highly scientific, nor for that matter, highly intellectual. They provide a set of simple explanations of how bureaucracy engulfs our daily lives and how those perpetrating these acts are using IT's fabulous capabilities to reach their goal. This book is for ordinary readers if such a person exists.

Acknowledgements

- Throughout this book, you will see quite a few icons, smart art and digital shapes. They appear as figures with a sequential number. These are inserted into the text from the stock of icons and the like in Microsoft's Office 365 Word ©. The author acknowledges their source and usage. The comments with these icons are those of the author and are sometimes light-hearted and frivolous.
- Thank-you, **Claire Moore,** for introducing me to the term *Obstructive Bureaucracy.* This term is often used in the book. The book is often built around this term and the spectre that it creates in our minds. Whenever the phrase is used in this book, it appears in bold type. Thanks, Claire.
- Thank-you, **John Whitney CBE,** for sitting with me on a summer's evening, to be precise, the 20th September 2020. John, you coined the word *Clutteridge.* Whenever that word is used in this book, like **Obstructive Bureaucracy,** it appears in bold type. Thanks, John.

Clutteridge is a new word, and it describes what the bureaucrats create to practice and perfect **Obstructive Bureaucracy.** It's a fog whose purpose is to slow down and prevent real progress.

It's a new word, and if had it been forged by Shakespeare, it would have been unopposed, written with a quill pen in dark ink and by now be part of our language today. But today, as it is novel and new (as far as we know), it is potentially subjected to all sorts of questions like:

- Is it legal?
- Does it offend anyone or any cause or organisation?
- Is it patented or copyrighted? Should it be?
- Does it conform to any known standards?
- Can money be made from its use?
- What does it mean?
- When will it be in a dictionary or a spellchecker?
- Is it a word comparable with *runcible?*[8]

Questions galore and answers a few. Perhaps that's where we are in humankind's journey to where we don't know we're going?

---

[8] See later references to Edward Lear and his writings.

Abstract of the book

This book discusses what part bureaucracy plays in the grand economic scheme of things. Why does an advanced country like the UK have meagre growth rates despite its educated population? This book is not an economics manual. It is about how bureaucracy, as practised by bureaucrats, aka Digital Icebergs in the book, is harnessing the capabilities of Information Technology (IT) to smother the real benefits of IT. Of course, these benefits are driven by the ever-increasing capabilities and affordability of the microchip and digital storage. The chip's part in providing information through the ages is first discussed in more than one form. Then how growth in the Information Age in which we live is dampened and hindered using the very capabilities that should be firing it up. This book is a readable discussion for anyone seeking a better understanding of our current lifestyle and how we are missing some of the benefits of the technology that we have evolved.

Examples of bureaucracy, or as the book calls it, **Obstructive Bureaucracy** abound. The book describes how chips portrayed information in stone, how information was then presented on parchment and paper. And how information is now presented everywhere through digital channels. It is these channels, whether for commercial or personal usage, that are being subjected to bureaucracy. The purpose of such a hindrance is to slow down progress by consuming productive time.

Bureaucracy has been with humankind since time began. With the advent of IT and the Information Age, it is flourishing like never. IT is enabling this!

3. About the author

Maurice J Perks is an Honorary Doctor of Science at Aston University, Birmingham, UK. The university where he obtained a B Sc. degree in physics many years ago. But his primary career after that was in computing. What we now call IT.

He was an IBM employee from 1968 until 2010. He was the first professional from the IBM Services Division to attain the IBM Fellow's coveted level in 2002.

He has spent fifty years working on the challenges of large and complex IT systems at deep development levels within the IBM Corporation and directly with many of the world's largest enterprises. At first, the systems he worked on were called computer systems, next data processing systems and now IT systems. He still calls them computer systems. Many of the systems that he worked upon were in the business world of finance. He has seen these systems' technology components increase in power and capability by order of countless levels. He's seen these systems evolve from isolated batch processes into the global connectivity of the Internet and the highly-coupled systems that ubiquitous and economic connectivity has enabled. He's seen the apparent complexity of systems increase by what feels to be many orders of magnitude.

Throughout his career, he has continuously sought to find a mathematical way of representing complexity. He has not succeeded because, at heart, he's an engineer instead of a scientist or philosopher. He passionately believes in what he calls *proper engineering*. He believes that our Universe has been appropriately engineered, and this is continuing. But, we may be interfering with the Big Program that governs us.

He is:

- A retired IBM Fellow
- A Fellow of the British Computer Society (BCS)
- A Fellow of the Institute of Engineering and Technology (IET)
- A former Royal Academy of Engineering Visiting Professor at the University of York
- He gives one day of his time each week to help at an IT walk-in centre in the UK where anyone can bring in an IT device and ask for advice.
- He still gets involved in complex IT projects. Usually, projects that are 'in trouble' through optimistic planning need 'reality' attention.

- He has co-authored a book entitled, Solving the Dynamic Complexity Dilemma

He lives with his wife, a pianist, in Dorset, UK and Nice, France. He comments that in Nice, the food's flavour is better than in Dorset, but in Dorset, the beer's flavour is better than in Nice. But then, an engineer would say that.

4. Part 1 Obstructive Bureaucracy

The challenge of the chip and the Digital Icebergs

5. Background and Introduction

Abstract

In this chapter, we begin to introduce a discussion centred upon bureaucracy and progress in a very general manner. We go back into history. Going forward into history is for the brave and foolish, not for us.

As humans have evolved, we have become smarter and supposedly better concerning our intelligence and how we live, our lifestyles. The formation of what we now call industries is considered. How certain revolutionary technical events have driven changes in these industries' processes and characters.

Some thoughts about bureaucracy

Bureaucracy is one of those words that we use when we encounter a hindrance. The hindrance can be small or big in its effects on our desire to move forward in achieving something. We think of it as an opposing force, and this book often takes that position. But some definitions class it as an organisational construct that is positive in enabling good government and governance. We, therefore, have two opposing forces. We're into the realm of Newton's Third Law of Motion which roughly states that: *Action and Reaction are equal and opposite*. Alas, the forces, call them effects if you like, are not equal regarding bureaucracy's impact. They do not obey Mr Newton's rule.

The word bureaucracy is an English extension of the French word *bureau*. It seems to have a clutch of meanings like; desk, office, office block, or even some sort of group of persons who act as a governing body. The last of those is, for many of us, the most frightening and threatening. Especially scary when the group of persons is not apparent to us. It's governance *behind the scenes!* Authority from below the waterline. We'll explain the significance of the waterline soon.

Figure 9 We can block anything

If bureaucracy has a positive effect on our progress as a planet and our journey to the sunlit uplands of paradise, it is welcome. It is essential. If it has a negative effect, primarily if it drives us downwards towards Armageddon, it is most unwelcome. It is threatening. As we have said; bureaucracy is like a coin; it has two sides. Well, two sides and an edge.

Let us start by thinking of bureaucracy as some form of organisational construct that is sometimes in the open but sometimes hidden. Sometimes it is invisible. It sometimes aids us but often hinders our progress as a civilised species.

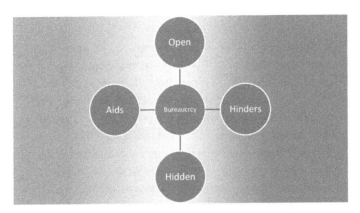

Figure 10 Basic attributes of bureaucracy

The good and the bad

As we often find, something has good and bad effects. Bureaucracy, as we have so far defined it is no exception. If we ask the question with the above diagram in mind, *what does bureaucracy do for us?* [9] We can combine each element and see the possible products.

Aids + Open	Good for real progress through proper organisation and processes.
Aids + Hidden	Good for progress even though activity is behind the scenes.
Hinders + Open	Not good for progress, but evident to all can be identified and 'attacked'. Like COVID-19, when understood and there is a vaccine available to all.
Hinders + Hidden	Not good for progress and very dangerous because it is behind the scenes and not evident. Like COVID-19 in the early days of the pandemic.

[9] This is a contortion of the well known question *What have the Romans ever done for us?* asked in the Monty Python Film The Life of Bryan 1979. For a sidetrack see Appendix B.

Bureaucrats are people who, when they see the light at the end of the tunnel, order more tunnel[10] – with thanks to John Quinton RAF Fighter Pilot, George Cross (1921 to 1951)

Our position in the Universe and perhaps beyond

We live on a small planet when it is compared to other heavenly bodies that we know exist. But our Earth is probably more giant in size and mass than the average body that makes up our Universe. We, the human beings that occupy our planet, and probably a host of other living species, think of ourselves as significant like our planet, prominent in the aspect of

Figure 11 Does size matter?

intelligence because we reason. We use our thinking minds to produce what we feel is a better world and a better lifestyle. We call this progress and now and again question our judgement. It's evolution. It's a journey. A journey through time or space and from where to where is not known so we can all forge our own opinions about the travel.

I think therefore I am – René Descartes (1596 to 1650) Thinker and mathematician

The journey is characterised because the majority feeling about each day is better than the day before. More weeks are better than the weeks before; more months are better than the months earlier, and so on. There are inevitable setbacks due to natural disasters, climate changes, pandemics and our human tendency to fight between ourselves. In 2020 we had a setback. But, despite these setbacks, the progress feels positive in an overall sense. We move forward in the

Figure 12 The trend is upward

direction of *better*. Members of each generation live longer and supposedly enjoy life more in terms of its quantity and quality. As a whole, our generation considers that we are better informed than a cave dweller with the Internet's advent. With the advent of 4G mobile phones, we are better connected than those who lived in the Middle Ages. In the end, better is a feeling, but on the whole, we do feel that life is better. You can debate the validity of this statement but avoid producing a form to assess the results.

---

[10] In fact Flight Lieutenant John Alan Quinton (GC DFC) actually used the word *Politicians* but here we have sunstituted the word *Bureaucrats*.

Remember, tomorrow is a good day. Tomorrow, you will maybe find everything will be much better than today. Captain Sir Tom Moore – Inspirational optimist (1920 to 2021)

OK, you may not think that it's better, but you cannot do anything other than agree that tomorrow will be different from today. You wait and see.

Patience is a virtue.

We are becoming smarter through progress.

Somehow we have become what is termed *smarter*. What *smarter* means varies from individual to individual, but perhaps that's part of the challenge or is the hidden beauty of the word and its meaning. It's not precise like a mathematical formula; it's open to intelligent consideration and personal feelings. Individuals can be smart. Groups of individuals operating as organisations can be smart; governments can be smart. The whole human race or other species can be smart. The brightness of the smartness increases, just like when the brightness of a lamp is increased.

Figure 13 Follow the light

Wisdom is our power to put our time and our knowledge to the proper use – Thomas J Watson (1874 to 1956), founder of IBM

As humankind evolved, he and she began to fuel the greater community's progress rather than just provide for herself or himself as an individual. This we now call productiveness and measure it as productivity. Perhaps in the very early days of the cave dwellers, it could mean that an individual made tools for others. It might mean that a group of men hunted wild animals, killed them and provided food for the women and children of the tribe back at the caves. As time moved on, it might be that a woman at a primitive loom could produce enough cloth to clad her whole family. The faster she worked, the more productive was her existence. The family gained from her productivity significantly when she increased it through effort and the use of new, as then, technology. Technology or better tooling, as we shall see, is key to a better existence and progress.

If everyone is moving forward together, then success takes care of itself – (Henry Ford, industrialist 1863 to 1947)

Industries and revolutions

As workers grouped themselves, industries grew, and the productivity of a

 specific class of work became recognised as a measure of industrial progress. No doubt, blacksmiths' productivity to produce swords and spears was monitored and recorded at times of conflict. Then in a remote and quiet corner of England in the 18th century, something historic and symbolic in the technology space happened. What we now know of as The Industrial

Figure 14 Full steam ahead

Revolution started. Not only did life begin to change for almost everyone and for everywhere on our planet, but the rate of change accelerated. Thereby progress increased by what was eventually to become leaps and bounds. What started in Shropshire in the UK became global because it was progressive and did make the world change. It was unstoppable even by the bureaucrats of those times.

That Industrial Revolution was, of course, the first one, and there have been, depending on who you read and who you believe, several more since that one. We can, for our purposes of discussion here, state that there have been three and perhaps we are in the process of a fourth:

1. First Industrial Revolution characterised by the use of Steam.
2. Second Industrial Revolution characterised by the use of Electricity.
3. Third Industrial Revolution characterised by the use of Computers.
4. Fourth Industrial Revolution characterised by the use of *to be decided.*

We'll discuss the *to be decided* space later in this book; until then, we'll temporarily say with anticipation; *watch this space.* If you can't wait, you can fill the space with *information.* So let's progress.

The age-old age

Each revolution causes humankind to experience a new age or at least humanity to define and designate a new era. There's nothing new about this since ages have been around since the dawn of time, whenever that was? There have been Ice Ages, a Stone Age and a Bronze Age, to mention a few that are easy to spell correctly. Some of these ages, like the last Ice Age, are characterised by natural changes. Humankind's smartness characterises some like the Bronze Age to use her or his brains to make progress. There wasn't a revolution per se as described above, but there was a significant change. Ages that are defined by human-inspired changes as a general rule do not end because something doesn't work anymore, or something runs out (well, not as yet?). A more advanced age supersedes them. For instance, it has been quoted that; *the Stone Age didn't end because we ran out of stone.* And we can say that the Bronze Age didn't end because it was no longer possible to make bronze.

Nothing lasts forever but at least we got these memories – J. Cole, Rapper singer (born 1985)

Once again, for our current discussion, we can say that we are in the Information Age that has happened because the computer was conceived, evolved and became ubiquitously affordable. In particular, because the microchip was created, developed and became ubiquitously affordable. We'll discuss the microchip or for short chip and its place in the current age and revolution later, but at last, the word chip has now been used in the body text of this book.

Figure 15 Chips with everything

Conclusion of this chapter

As human beings, we've come a long way down the winding highway known as wisdom. At first, the progress was slow, but now we are hurtling along at dramatic speeds. These speeds are continuously increasing. Whether this is good or bad is debatable and with it, whether we are becoming smarter is debatable. Whatever smarter means? Both in direction and speed, our current velocity is driven by the microchip and its unlimited usage. Uses for good or bad is the question, so read on, please.

As this book unfolds, you will encounter the following icon in several places with brief wording below. It represents a pyramid of people with, for instance, the most or unusual at the top, the most common at the bottom. This configuration is how you can often see the makeup of society in terms of leaders and followers. Or the movers and shakers and those who don't.

When an individual is subjected to bureaucracy, they feel in the pyramid of life. It is as though they are bearing the weight of bureaucracy on their shoulders. This configuration is how layers of government can feel to a citizen. Without getting too deeply into politics, imagine that you are a citizen in a small town somewhere in a nation that is part of the EU. Imagine the layers above you and the potential points of contact that you, as a citizen, have to experience not essential law or administration but the excess bureaucracy that uses up your time and patience. The same may be true of the Federal and State administrations of the USA. Imagine it in your own country.

Governments serve the people. The people are servants of their governments.

There's something wrong with the above statement. It's like a contradictory equation. Its two sides are both equal and unequal.

6. A short and narrow history of IT

Abstract

This chapter is kept short to avoid the feel of bureaucracy as you might expect; we briefly consider the history of what we today call Information Technology (IT).

IT has changed and transposed itself as individual pieces of the technologies on which it is built and have matured. It has become affordable and has been designed and engineered into the business and social systems we experience and use today. Systems we share and benefit from as we live in what we are calling the IT Age.

The dates quoted in this chapter are given as rough guides. You can change them if you think that they are not exact.

Computing

The subject we call Information Technology (IT) and as we know it today has not always been named IT. It's part of technology evolution. The foundations existed long ago. Firstly in the middle of the 20th century, we had computing or, more precisely, commercial computing and scientific computing.

The primary purpose of scientific computing was to crunch numbers and solve

complex equations through execution speed. Computers were faster than humans when executing mathematics. The scientific branch of computing was number-focused, and we often heard about number crunching. Suddenly calculating π to one hundred decimal-places was possible even though the exact answer to 101 decimal-places wasn't clear. One of the basic building blocks of

Figure 16 At last we have liftoff

sending rockets to the moon on a specific path had appeared as a tool in humankind's toolbox. Scientific computing was, and still is, a powerful and essential tool in many forms of engineering and science.

Commercial computing's primary function was to automate manual clerical tasks and provide necessary information about what had been going on. Inputs were slow. Data storage was minimal and expensive compared with today's economics. Inputs and outputs were typically paper-based[11]. The paper

---

[11] Paper punch cards or paper tape for input. Printed listings for output.

medium is the direct descendant of stone tablets, papyrus and hides. Information was restricted to sequential listings or summary reports. Costs were high, and the benefits often debatable. The whole scene was very business-oriented, usually large enterprise business-oriented. The entry costs were too high for small businesses though they could join sharing schemes that allowed them some first steps into the new world.

Operatives executing input processes looked at input forms which were often tightly defined with an input box for each character. Free-format for input data or output information was rare. The design of the interfaces was fixed design. It was rigid and tightly-defined, so there was no chance for customisation and personal preferences. Quite a lot of what we now call legacy still exists, and the challenge to change remains. It's Brownfield rather than the Greenfield of the new stuff. Ploughing a new furrow can be a harrowing experience.

Figure 17 Plouging is a harrowing experience

Very roughly for this discussion, we can say that the Computing Age (Digital) was from 1950 to 1970. It did exist before 1950, and computing certainly didn't finish at the 1970 date, but that span of 20 years is when it was blossoming.

> **I think there will be a world market for maybe 5 computers[12] –** Thomas J Watson (1874 to 1956)

Data Processing

The Data Processing (DP) phase was a period that we can think of as data-centric as computing systems' storage capabilities increased. The data analysis was becoming more extensive. More information was being derived from the greater depth and width of the data passing through the operational systems. Some inputs and outputs were in real-time and were now beginning to be screen-based with network connections. Screens, usually with monochromatic green backgrounds and limited white text formatting, displayed data inputted from a keyboard. They also showed output information in a limited text format and elementary graphical images in specific parts of the screen's geometry.

Figure 18 I'm green with envy

---

[12] Thomas Watson is said to have made this statement (or under statement) in 1943 but the author whose career in IBM was from 1968 until 2010 never met anyone who heard him say this, nor anyone who had met anyone who heard him say it. Perhaps he did, perhaps he didn't.

Finally, the hereditary link with the tablets of stone and the more flexible parchment and paper style media was broken. In a subsequent chapter, we

discuss stone tablets and paper and there use as information sources. But with early IT, a link was broken. It was becoming noticeable that inputs were now more manageable. The devices on which they were made held a promise of greater flexibility. Some non-expert in the technology business end-users were now able to input their data and see their outputs. We shall later call

Figure 19
Spring is here

the Digital Icebergs as well as bureaucrats. This, for them, was a vision of bureaucracy's sunlit uplands. The shoots of something big in the journey to their bureaucratic heaven appeared. Progress was being made on their road to hades and the fires of hell. Costs were still high, and the whole scene was business-oriented as regards usage and affordability. The systems were part of business life and not everyday personal life.

Very roughly for this discussion, we can say that the Data Processing Age was from 1970 to 2000. Of course, data was being processed long before 1970 and up to the present time. Still, that span of 30 years is when it was blossoming and bearing some fruit before it was superseded by what we now know as the IT age.

Information Technology (IT)

IT is a general term covering a wide range of:

- physical devices,
- connections,
- processes,
- programs,
- technology architectures,
- frameworks,
- data,
- skills
- services and
- a lot more.

Information Technology, IT encompasses how the likes of these examples listed here are engineered together and used.

*Figure 20
Cloudy
forecast*

In the 1990s, a set of technologies were maturing both in capability and cost affordability. It's debatable whether this was a grand design from somewhere on our planet, in the Universe or beyond? Or was it by chance? We can use another list of the critical technologies we have amalgamated to form the IT Age infrastructure. They include but are by no means a complete list so the informed reader can add other entries. Any reader reading this list a few months after it has gone into print can add to it because this is how IT evolves. Nothing stands still. So a possible and dated list:

- The microchip in power, cost, reliability and size.[13]
- Fibre optic networks and associated bandwidth connectivity and throughput.
- Ubiquitous wireless (wi-fi) connectivity, publically and domestically.
- Cheap storage (cost per Mbyte) to store data, whatever and wherever.
- Search engines to find information based upon flexible search criteria in a common language.
- A global population of IT engineers to design and build systems and components.
- A global population of educated programmers to produce applications (apps) for many types of devices and business and personal uses.
- Cheap portable devices like laptops, tablets, smartphones within the affordability of the general public's purses, wallets and credit cards.
- Amazingly detailed output screens with excellent resolution and highly responsive reactions to changing picture formats. Great graphics.
- The order of the Internet (IP addressing) and the World Wide Web (WWW). Sort of by design but not by a bureaucracy; else, we would still be paper-based.

You can add to the above list from your own experiences and your views of the IT Age. Some entries in the list depend upon others in the list, like programming uses microchips for its execution. Search engines are functionally programming. As a generalism, the parts for the business and personal systems that we know today came together and formed real systems that can operate anywhere globally. And can be used by many, many users.

In this IT Age, the user interface was moved from inside businesses to the general public. A member of which can be anywhere on our planet or sometimes beyond. Anyone providing a retail or financial service soon realised that the channels to their marketplaces had changed in width, depth and time, especially service-open times. Sometimes security was forgotten, though. Businesses and the general public have seen the change as a progressive step

---

[13] It's interesting to note also as regards heat output since this has been one of the challenges of chips from their early days. Too much heat output dissipated because of the power usage and the chips become fried.

in their lifestyles. Unless security has been ignored, both parties see the easy access of all kinds of information to benefit. Vast quantities of knowledge have been stored, and access to it is often open to all at no direct cost. Processes are immediate or close to real-time. The benefits seem to be endless, and they usually are affordable. The supply of the base technology and its yearly improvement seems endless as well. The sunny uplands seem to have been reached.

Figure 21 All is not as it seems

But there is a fly in the digital, both the commercial and economic, ointment. We might have known it so to be[14]. That intruder can best be classed as an opposing force and is, of course, bureaucracy. Beauroacracy being practised as a dark and black art. We'll discuss this in a chapter that follows.

There's no reason for any individual to have a computer in their home – Ken Olsen CEO DEC 1977[15]

Conclusion of this chapter

IT, in its broadest form, is about 70 years old. It has evolved from an expensive and very localised subject and set of practices to a global activity. In essence, all of this means that everyone on our planet is connected to everyone else on our planet. Everyone has access to most of the information that our planet knows about. IT is everywhere for everyone. We live in a joined-up world, and it's based upon the chip and the uses that it has been put to by some pretty bright technical and commercial minds.

---

[14] Alternative spelling *bee*
[15] DEC (Digital Equipment Corporation) never did become a big player in PCs and smartphones. One day sometime this statement may become true if society rejects the intrusion of 'computers' into the homes and distrust their intentions.

7. What is information?

Abstract

In this chapter, the reader is informed about how information has existed in different ages in different forms. Of course, it exists today in what we can call a digital format in what we are calling the Digital Information Age. That's the short information about this chapter. More would have involved time-wasting. Time wasting is a prime attribute of the very bureaucracy we are trying to eliminate. So without delay, let us start.

A starting definition

We can start by postulating that information is that which informs us. That

Figure 22 On your marks

seems evident, so the question now is; informs us of what though and with what effects? The answer to this next question involves a long debate. Still, this book's contents and flow are a starting definition that will be refined as the book proceeds. Still, as we have said already, the main effect is that information is increasingly playing in bureaucracy, or perhaps more accurately, the other way around. On the reverse of the coin even further, that part that bureaucracy plays in the information surrounding us.

Information is right for you sometimes

When we experience a piece of information visually or audibly and absorb it to some degree, the absorption can make us wiser, smarter, and happier. It can confuse us, frustrate us, make us angry, and worry us, not to mention it can misinform us if the information is misinformation.

Information is often an aggregation of data, as we'll discuss in chapter 7, and distributed constructed to tell us, or show us, something specific. For instance, it might be the balance of a bank account, a news item, a dictionary definition of what a word like information means, the contents of an email or the weather forecast at where we are. Today, everywhere you look and listen, you see and hear information often digitally delivered to us whether we asked for it to be delivered or not. Our world is indeed *information-rich*. Too rich, some might say, opulent, some might say. If you are obese and overeat, it's relatively easy to go on a diet. Well, for a day! Still, it's less easy to restrict the information put in front of you and that you consume directly or indirectly.

Nothing is new

It's easy in our digital world to assume that information, construction, and provision have come about in our current age and are part of the Third Industrial Revolution. Is this true or false?. There is no doubt that this age has seen spectacular progress in data storage, data analysis, and information presentation at a myriad of end-user interfaces. There has been a degree of progress beyond the wildest dreams of even the greatest minds of the mid-1900s. Every couple of years or so, something doubles. The multiplier is big. Has anything so rapid been experienced in a former age? Yet, snippets of information have been seen, heard and absorbed by the human race, and perhaps other species way before any of the Industrial Revolutions that we have identified.

Figure 23 Times 2

We're now going to go back into history. Going back into history is a wise move. If you go forward into history, you are predicting and forecasting that is a chancy business. Many mistakes are made that you will probably know what will happen if you take the opposite of the prediction. So we'll go back in time.

Figure 24 Someone must know why I exist?

Information through the ages

Firstly, in times so long ago as to be longer than long ago, pieces of information will have been passed from one cave dweller to another. Past perhaps in a series of grunts and shakes of a stick-like club. Some might attest that much of our so-called current digital information is no better than this or even regression from this format. A lot of the information that we receive is akin to a series of grunts. As well as grunts, cave paintings gave cave dwellers information and these paintings are more permanent than a series of grunts. The cave paintings at Lascaux in the Dordogne of France[16] are examples of this type of information from way back. The writing with its inbuilt information was, and sometimes still is, literally *on the wall.*

A few thousand years ago, humankind began to take stone pieces and reduce them to a manageable size to be easily handled. A craftsman of the time started to chip out messages in the faces of the stone. This was again information being presented to the end-user. The production was a slow process, but some of its methods and products have often lasted for centuries.

---

[16] They predate the aforementioned French Postal Service (La Poste)

Will today's modern and up-to-date procedures and products do likewise? Only time will tell again.

Eventually, the forerunners of what we today know as paper were processed and used; papyrus, parchment and animal hides. Such mediums are both flexible and light in weight. So scrolls and then books were inscribed and became the prime sources of textual information until the latter half of the 20th century. Canvas paintings bore pictorial information. But the production of these types of information substrate was laborious. We can only assume error-prone with no way of backspacing to erase an error like we have today. If you got something wrong, you had to start again with a new piece of your chosen medium and take more care. Productivity in today's terms was probably low.

Figure 25 The writing came off the wall

Progress in the production of the written information source was then made in a giant leap; that leap was the invention and engineering of the printing press. This occurred in 1439 or 1440 when a blacksmith and goldsmith named Johannes Gutenberg (1400 to 1468) pressed the first printing press in Germany into action. In more ways than one, he forged a revolution. Now the media of information distribution like pages and books of pages could be produced at a rate that hundreds and hundreds of scribes could not match. The accuracy problem was also partially solved. We'll return to the combination of speed and accuracy again.

Books go viral and everywhere.

Information distribution was now what we might call *viral* compared with the previous ways. This was real progress, especially when the industrialisation of the manufacture of printing presses happened. It was akin to the industrialisation of computers' manufacture in the second half of the 20th century. Suppose more significant quantities of a product are needed. In that case, this can be done by making more instances of the product's production means. If A is made by B and you want to make more A's, make more B's capable of producing more A's.[17]

Figure 26 A new leaf was turned over

Gutenberg did something utterly fantastic in terms of the enablement of enlightenment and the advancement of religions, science, and technologies. Would Sir Isaac Newton (1643 to 1727) have pushed our world forwards through the

---

[17] There's an engineering example of this in Appendix A

general availability of his printed scientific laws a hundred plus years earlier? Or William Shakespeare (1564 to 1616) entertained such a broad audience with his printed plays and poems less than a hundred years later? As often happens in and around our planet, there is a dark cloud for every silver lining. That dark cloud is that Gutenberg provided the bureaucrats of that age and the ages after that with a beautiful tool to execute their craft's dark sides. He laid the ground for the existence of *the printed form,* the form to be filled in, about which we'll begin a discussion about later.

Trying to be more correct, it seems to be true that in Asia, China probably,

Figure 27 Not really technically interesting

early manual presses made of wood were operational before Gutenberg's breakthrough. Still, somehow it doesn't seem fitting that a revolution can be based upon something wooden. Wood doesn't give one a sense of technical achievements like stone and metal and their associated processes. It's a fact that the world-famous Stonehenge circle of rocks[18] on the Wiltshire Plane of the UK has near to it the remains of a henge that was made from wood, the Woodhenge. However, few get excited about its existence like they do Stonehenge, given its technical splendours and supposed construction dates.

Something that is quite obviously not obvious

It is now interesting to halt the above discussion and make a simple but almost entirely overlooked observation. That observation is that we have encountered the word *chip* in the words of this book. How strange that those information portrayers of long ago would be the forefathers and foremothers of today's microchip engineers. The digital information experts use their products and skills to provide us with information. Imagine an operative with the stone in front of him or her. With a chisel in one hand, they were chipping away, producing a lot of chips. Information as created then depended upon chips or holes where chips had been. Information as produced today depends upon chips. Chips of a very different kind, of course, but wait, there may be something else that binds the ages together and unites the two forms of chips.

---

[18] They are called stones but are rocks by origin.

That something is the chemical element silicon (Si and atomic number 14). Suppose the ancient writer and chipper chipped into granite or sandstone. In that case, silicon is a constituent of granite in the form of silicate, a combination of silicon (1 instance) and oxygen (4 instances). Microchips, or for our discussion chips, have as their raw elemental component silicon. Despite research to displace silicon with other elementary components like in the stone tablets and other larger objects of old, the silicon factor remains the bridge upon which information portrayal depends throughout the ages.

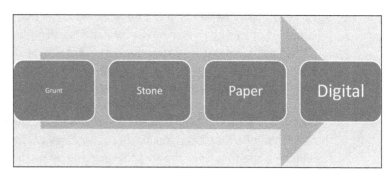

Figure 28 Sand gets everywhere

Conclusion of this chapter

Information is about informing us about something. Though we live in the IT Age, information has been around since time began. If you believe in some of the ways that the Universe happened before time began, it has been around longer. Today data is being created and captured at an alarming rate. Chips are everywhere, making the capture possible and are being used as the tool to produce information. We are in a technology sandstorm.

Suppose you want to summarise how the key mediums that have and are used to portray information we can say that there have been three. Digital hasn't replaced paper, as yet, but may do. The diagram below is not to scale. Digital includes screens, sound, and a growing set of strange eyeglasses and helmets.

We know where we have been but do not know where we are going.

| Grunt | Stone | Paper | Digital |

Figure 29 Information mediums over the years..

8. How information is manufactured, stored and distributed

Abstract

This chapter starts with an outline description of how data is created. Then the reader is informed about how it can become information. This briefly covers the distinction between scientific numbers and commercial characters, and textual data. It recaps on the history of information and the fashions concerning how information can be provided have progressed. How data and information have been, and is, stored is discussed and how information is distributed to end-users who may or may not want it.

The manufacturing process of information

Raw data

To understand how information is formed, we'll reuse a simple model of a physical product's manufacture. In this model, components, assemblies, parts, pieces, and raw materials are assembled to a specific design. A finished physical product of some kind is the output. The natural ingredient of information is data. Sometimes the more data, the better; other times, it is the opposite, as we shall see.

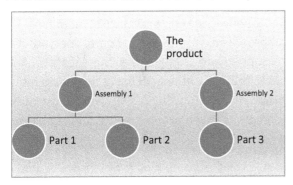

Figure 30 A simple product

Very simply, if we have pieces of data designated by Dn and assemble them in a specific way, then they become a piece of information (In).

$$D1 \ \& \ D2 \ \& \ D3 \ \& \ D4 \rightarrow In$$

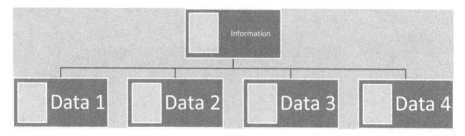

Figure 31 Information from data

Or specifically using real numbers as the base data and the information that we want is the sum of the series then simple additions give us:

$$1 + 2 + 3 + 4 \rightarrow \text{In} = 10$$

If the information we want is to know the highest number in the series, the specific way changes and becomes more complex. Analysis has to be done on the numbers to determine the biggest:

$$1 < 2 < 3 < 4 \rightarrow \text{In} = 4$$

If you have, let us say a pamphlet that describes how to make something in the pre-digital ages. The information produced was merely raw data. The output equalled the input. Names were chipped into stone tablets. Messages were scribed onto parchment or the like. The skills were in defining the messages and scribing them onto the appropriate medium. These skills were those of the early information engineers or sometimes even prophets with unique abilities.

Combining data and raw information

Over time, intelligent persons would think of combining raw data pieces into a piece of derived information. For example, if a shepherd had 100 sheep in one pasture and 100 sheep in another pasture, he or she could say I have 2 flocks of sheep rather than saying that he or she had 200 sheep. In this instance, a flock being 100 sheep. They might also say that they had 800 sheeps' feet, having counted the sheep and checked that each sheep had 4 feet. The raw input data was 100 sheep and 100 sheep, but the output was 200 sheep, 2 flocks, or 800 feet. The depth of information and its complexity was evolving. This continues, of course. Suddenly we are confronted with the modern version of the count of sheep's feet without understanding why and grasping the real significance of why there has been a change.

Information about the 2020 COVID-19 pandemic state and progress was a classic example of confusing and misleading information. There was data galore. There was derived information galore about how many infections there were, how many hospitalisations there were, and how many deaths there were. Not much on how the virus was being transmitted from person to person. Not where the virus was being transmitted. The resultant confusion and nervousness were considerable. So normally sensible persons were worried and confused. There was what we could call *Information Chaos*.

Briefly summarising, raw data is transformed into information through analysis and derivation and information results. It's as simple or complex as that.

Numbers lead the way

As time on the information scale progressed, what we now know as mathematics improved and some basic tools to support the new ways of calculating were developed. The abacus with its counting frames. The slide rule with its analogies of length to numbers. Then various so-called engines like The Difference Engine that was designed and constructed by Charles Babbage[19] (1791 to 1871) in 1822 appeared. This early computer was a mighty piece of precision engineering by a real Progressive. It was so impressive that in 1823 the UK government awarded Babbage £1700 to engineer the next version. Today the new version of even a humble smartphone costs many, many times more than that. At that time, one of today's pounds sterling was equivalent to about one-hundredth of a pound then. That's inflation for you to consider. So £1700 is roughly £170,000 as of today. It seems clear that the Progressives outsmarted what we will call in a future chapter the Iceberg Bureaucrats of the time. It's worth recognising that the UK was in the grips of the Steam Industrial Revolution that was fuelling growth. Whether the resulting wealth was fairly distributed is a matter for debate.

In the 19th century and into the 20th century, the push of science and

mathematics was dominating the analytical scene. Books were becoming commonplace, but the great minds wanted to crack some of the challenges of numeric data that were too longwinded to unravel employing paper and pen, or even primitive calculators. The faster you could crunch numbers with a formula that defined the rules, the quicker you had the answer

Figure 32 This is not a piece of cake

as useful information. Today on an elementary tablet device, you can compute

---

[19] It's possible to note that Charles Babbage was tutored and helped on the work of his Difference Engine by a writer and mathematician named Ada Lovelace. The British Computer Society (BCS) each year holds sponsors and Lovelace Lecture. In 2008 the author gave the Lovelace Lecture entitled; Why IT Projects Fail.

the cube root of 2 to 14 decimal places as 1.25992104989287 in an instance. Now try the same using paper and pen. You can use the Internet to find the 'manual' techniques if you don't know them. Please return here to this point in this book. You will probably have been away from it for over one year in doing the calculation. When you have done the calculation, you have probably made a mistake. The attributes of speed and accuracy that showed promise and dominate our IT systems today were being explored and exploited.

Data Processing becomes of age, information explodes

Let us stand-back and reposition our discussion by looking at what we have stated to this point and solidifying that.

The position was taken that three ages of what we today call IT have and are existing: Computing, Data Processing, and IT. Data capture was becoming automated in the Data Processing Age as transactions were processed often immediately in real-time. The number of places within a business process where data could be captured increased rapidly. The amount of information going out of systems increased and overtook the amount of data going in when measured simply by the number of characters. The amounts of data stored soared, and the desire to explore these oceans of data was in the same traditions as humankind's desire to explore our planet in previous centuries. The labels tagged to each style of data evolution and information are akin to clothes fashion eras. The types were a fashion statement. Many false and overly-enthusiastic claims were made as to the great leaps and bounds that were possible. Jumps in the direction of perfect forecasting, prediction, fraud detection and the complete explanation of the Universe and all its contents.

The techniques, or more appropriately fashionable ways, to explore the data evolved under such banners as:

- Management Information.
  - A simple analysis of lists of sequential or indexed data for businesses only. What you get is what you see, sort of.
- Data Warehousing.
  - An attempt to make data and the delivery of information feel like a retail warehouse. If it's in stock, find it and send it. We'll find it for you.
- Data Mining.

- An attempt to make the exploration of data and the extraction of information appear like the deep shaft mining of minerals. We'll dig deep.
- Big Data.
  - As lots and lots of data were produced, the excitement of its size and potential was hyped to titanic proportions. Alas, the golden egg of Big Information has not accrued. It still might, but then fashions fade. The expectations are significant, the results disappointing.
- Now Artificial Intelligence (AI), or parts of it.
  - The jury is out on this, human or android. The evidence of success is sketchy. But it seems that today if anyone wants funding for any project to reveal anything that any human cannot show, the project must have an AI label on it. Yes, AI is a big business rather than Big Data and Big Information which are yesterday's fashions.

Each of the above has its specific organisational style of data and its ways of analysing data and producing information. Also, each has its expertise and advocates. It's interesting to note that to sell the concepts of exploring data set out above, those who named them resorted to using industrial and manufacturing terminology. Terms such as warehouse and mining so that business persons could have a known model in their minds of the playing field. The outputs were always Management Information, though. Well, until Personal Information entered the scene.

As a normal part of much information-retrieval is the simple Keyword searching facility. The end-user can search with what seems to be as many word combinations as possible and get the search results exactly or fuzzily. For instance, Newton's search will give the hits on Sir Issac Newton and may also provide the hits on Newtown with the explanation; Did you mean Newtown? But the input language is wordy and everyday-speak, and not some complex digital syntax that you have to learn and then forget and learn again.

Figure 33
I see no dips

How is information stored?

We have discussed that data, the raw material of information, was stored on media like stone tablets, hides, parchments, and eventually proper paper from times long ago. In these forms, or is it, on these forms, the data was raw and as-is, or as-was. It could be collated into books, and these became increasingly available in civilised societies. National libraries had existed since ancient times. The oldest library we know of is the al-Qarawiyyin library in Fez, Morocco. Like many libraries, these institutions were and still are, associated with a seat of learning. In the 19th century, local libraries became places where anyone could go, find and ingest information. The storage was still only on paper, mainly within books that eventually were indexed so that anyone could find information faster. Indexing became an essential aspect of information storage and retrieval.

At the start of the 19th century[20] in France, one of those leaps that drive the technology curve happened. Joseph Marie Jacquard (1752 to 1834) demonstrated the Jacquard loom that incorporated the Jacquard engine, a system of linked cards, each of which had holes punched in designated places. The sequence of these holes was what we can think of as a program. They governed the loom's execution in the same way that a program regulates a computer's execution today. What Jacquard had done was to start a fundamental movement in the capture, storage and analysis of data. He had started digitisation. He didn't know it, of course, because, like so many steps forward, the extent of the importance of his effort was not realised immediately. Time is a beautiful revealer of success or failure.

Figure 34 The race is off so it's now on

Digitisation

The digitisation of a number, a set of numbers, a character, a set of characters, a picture, a sound means that something has been transformed into a pattern of zeros and ones. A pattern that can be 'understood' by a computer. The 'understood' means that it can be input to a computer and have a specific meaning. The something is codified. Its code is understood by a particular computer with what we can call a specific and defined architecture.

In those early days, so little data was digitised. This state persisted until the second half of the 20th century, as discussed in the chapter: A short and narrow history of IT. But then the curve began to make a real upturn until our present-day. Now anyone can guess how much of the data of our civilised world is digitised and stored. Of course, the answer is closing in on 100% through two factors; the first is to digitise all existing data. The second is that we are producing enormous quantities of new data; its only state is digital. We

---

[20] Probably 1801.

are monitoring more and more of our happenings and activities with digital recording and analysis. We are increasingly digital, whatever that implies.

All this data is available to be analysed and collated into information and supposedly drive our civilisation forward. It is readily there for us to increase our knowledge and wisdom. We have repeatedly also said our productivity and wealth. But one of the great imponderables about our existence is defined by the uncertainty of anything being certain.

There's a relationship between our KNOWLEDGE, our WISDOM and our EVOLUTION as a species. No doubt, someday, some wise person will produce an equation that tells us mathematically what this relationship is. There's a great probability that the equation will be so complex that only a minimal set of our species will have the wisdom to understand it. So until then, and probably long after now, we can have a simple diagram which is, of course, is not drawn to any scale.

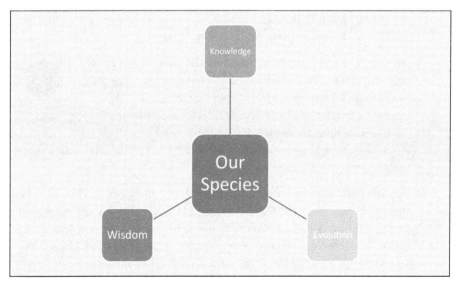

Figure 35 Please explain further if you can

Nothing is so simple as it cannot be misunderstood – Freeman Teague Jr., CEO of The Leadership Trust

Physical storage brought up to date

We have discussed the storage or recording as a more appropriate word, data, and information on various media forms. Even with early computers, the storage media were slow and expensive. These media were also prone to malfunction and even perhaps the destruction or corruption of the recorded contents. Data destruction was a common occurrence, so everything was backed-up to compensate. Examples of these media of storage are:

1. Punched cards with holes
   - Usually 80 columns per card, thereby 80 characters per card. Any number of cards per input deck.
2. Paper tape with holes
   - Any length up to what could be physically handled. Thereby any number of characters.
3. Magnetic tape
   - Any length up to what could be stored on a physical reel. Many characters.
4. Direct Access Storage (DASD)
   - From a few Kilobytes to many Terabytes over time.
   - Part of a mainframe computer, server, PC or laptop
5. Solid-State Memory
   - Many Gigabytes
   - Part of a smartphone, tablet, PC, laptop

Numbers 1, 2 and 3 above were sequential recording devices with no indexing. To find data, you had to search through the media to find the precise data you wanted. As above, numbers 4 and 5 allow programs to directly access a specific piece of data through indexes and address structures. Once you have indices, you have made a significant step on the useful data ladder. The needle in the haystack has just become much more findable.

Figure 36 I'm in a spin

The cost reductions in storing data have been remarkable. In 1956 IBM shipped an early DASD called the IBM 350 as part of the IBM 305 RAMAC (Random Access Machine Accounting System), which had a maximum capacity of 20 million characters (20Mbytes). The cost was lots and lots of US Dollars, say $3000/month for a 5 million character version called *the beast*.

Today the cost of storage can be as low as $0.1/GByte/month, and by the time you read this passage in this book, it will be much less. The slalom of storage costs will have continued. And the costs often cover multiple copies of the same data so that if one copy is lost through physical corruption, then another copy is available.

The clouds are gathering

Storage used to be a part of the computer system with the storage devices connected to the processors by Input/Output (I/O) channels and physical

cables. Now only limited amounts of data are kept locally and attached to large and small computers. The data has often been migrated to The Cloud. In the Cloud, the data is distributed

Figure 37 I'm homeless

wherever is convenient across enormous storage configurations, duplicated or more in the number of copies of a specific piece of data. Connectivity is through high-speed pipes.

In short, data is now stored in The Cloud and is everywhere. It is accessible from everywhere on earth and beyond. Data and information are truly global, and probably beyond, but since we don't know where the boundaries of the Universe are, it is not sensible to say where the limits of this accessibility are. You don't know where your data is but your system, no matter how large or how small and personal does, you hope. It's a matter of trust.

How is information distributed?

What we have been discussing above is a request-driven information system that is it is end-user driven. The end-user is aware of the information and why the information is being presented to him or her. We might call this Solicited Information. There is another way that information is given to any of us. It is what we shall call Unsolicited Information.

Solicited Information

The information is manufactured for the end-user based upon the end-user's request, usually in realtime and almost instantaneously. Because the data is

preassembled and indexed, these systems' designers have anticipated the end-users keyword requests. The information is delivered to the end-user. The end-user is in control at the time of the request and the output's extent to a certain degree. The outcome may be pages and pages of references but is rarely

Figure 38 An orderly list

overwhelming. If it is, it is ordered to give the most probable answers first.

The seeker of the information may read a specific book to become educated on a particular topic. He or she may turn on a TV news program to become aware of the latest news happenings. They may open a book on a specific page to determine the current research state into a particular medical challenge. The output of such solicited enquiries may be padded-out with extras like advertisements and secondary information sources. Still, practically the whole process is predictable. It isn't encumbered with frustrating extra sub-processes and nonsense that the end-user has never contemplated and requested.

The seeker gets more or less what he or she is seeking.

Seek, and ye shall find.

Unsolicited Information

As you might expect, unsolicited information is delivered to an end-user who has not directly asked for it. He or she may have shown an interest in the information's general context but has not sent a specific and structured request for it. He or she may have looked at a holiday flight some days before and is now receiving a list of cheap flights to the desired destination and places nearby.

The seeker gets something that he or she is not seeking.

Don't seek, and ye shall be found.

The presentation of information

The presentation of information has always been part of human existence, as

discussed earlier, especially in the chapter; What is information? In terms of delivery, it has traditionally been when an individual or business person has requested it directly or has asked for a weekly report, let us say. But now, two factors mean that information is delivered to end-users at any time and with any frequency.

Figure 39 I know what I want

Firstly, we have already said mountains upon mountains of data available for analysis so that customised information can be directed anywhere the data collector and sender chooses. It might be a one-off, intermittent or what is known as streamed continuously. There is no shortage of content, derived content, or anticipated content like:

- She asked for this exact information before, so I'll send it again. And keep sending it.
- He has been looking at flights to Paris Orly, so I'll send him flights to Orly and Charles De Gaulle airports since they are all in the Paris region of France.
- This person asked for flights to Naples, Italy, so I'll send these and hotels in Naples, car hire and the web address of a site that offers competitive currency exchanges of UK Pounds to Euros.

The complexity of the information and how it is derived from the data available can grow and grow and grow until the recipient(s) are swamped with information, most of which was never requested. Patterns can be identified to determine that 24% of those requesting information about activity A asked for details on Activity B and eventually made a purchase of P. Increasingly, the depth of analysis and its conclusions appears to be endless. The additional information can grow and grow as the data grows and the research extends.

Most members of the human race have a limited capacity to absorb information. By the second, absorb by the hour, by the day, by the year, by a lifetime. Indeed our capacity peaks somewhere in our lifetime. Though we absorb more and more from experiences, it's doubtful that we absorb more and more from bombardment. You often hear the phrase *too much information*. An alarm bell of *information overload* rings out constantly. The Information Age is probably beginning to destroy itself like a kid in a candy store. Most people have a limited capacity for most things.

Conclusion of this chapter

Data is transformed into information through simple or complex analysis. Our ability to create digitised data is today extraordinary. The cost per unit of storing oceans and mountains of data is continuously decreasing. Whether we are analysing all of this data sensibly is not clear.

We often live with information overload, but there is no doubt that we are in the Information Age powered by the ever-powerful-cheaper chip. Some of the end-users are suffering from *Information Overload* and getting giddy, though. Excessive information is beginning to destroy the thirst for knowledge.

9. The types of Progress Players

Abstract

In this chapter, we define and discuss the types of humans that we call; the Progress Players. They affect the progress made towards a better world and, in the case of the UK's economic growth, significant positive upward movement on the graphs. Some types of these players have a positive effect. Some classes do not affect. Alas, some types have an apparent adverse effect. And, as we shall see, some types have a covert and hidden negative impact.

The types of progress players

To investigate progress versus retardation or forward versus backward concerning what we have discussed and may call *the state of enlightenment of the human race,* we will propose that the four categories are:

1. The Progressives.
2. The Neutrals.
3. The Luddites.
4. The Digital Icebergs

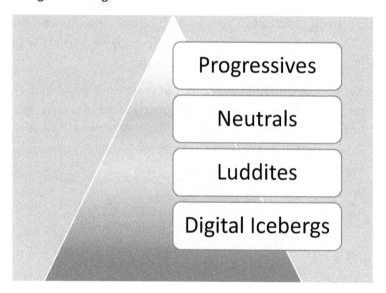

The above is the Pyramid of Bureaucratic Danger. Danger to real enlightenment and progress. The pyramid is not drawn to scale. We do need change if it does represent the distribution of our types.

We'll now take each one of these types and try to label them with their specific characteristics. It's not easy to say what percentage of each category is but an attempt is made to size this very roughly.

A guess is better than complete ignorance, I guess, but I don't know?

The Progressives

The Progressives is by far the most illustrious group. They are often famous in

history and standout as the creative thinkers and doers of our societies throughout the ages. Like any community, they form a triangle or hierarchy. They can be arranged in tiers regarding their order of effect within this category. For our purposes, we have three levels. At the top tier are scientists, writers, musicians, politicians, even military leaders who are household names and have added to our knowledge and existence through

Figure 40 Standing on shoulders

what they have left us as information that leads to increased enlightenment, usually in a written format: the likes of Newton, Einstein, JS Bach, Robert Noyce[21], Shakespeare. The list seems endless, but as a proportion of the human race throughout time, the list is short. They make the jumps. They usually work as individuals. Specifically, in the Digital Information Age that we are in, we might suddenly say, WOW, we've got the Internet and the World Wide Web! Let's call them geniuses. They make giant leaps possible.

They are the **Giant Antelopes** of our species. They have rare minds, exceptional minds which they apply to enormous effect.

Lower in the Progressive Pyramid and order is a layer of players who use the higher layer's information output to improve by significant factors the artefacts used by we humans. These are the engineering types who build significantly better *things and stuff*. They make step changes like twice-as-fast, twice as reliable, half the price, etc., happen. There are many of these at work as engineers, scientists, researchers, designers, etc. They usually work in small teams. Let us call them the Rolls-Royce Engineers of our specials, where the term Rolls-Royce is used in a very generic sense. They produce significant step changes.

Figure 41 Big jumpers

---

[21] One of the inventors of what we now call the microchip with the first integrated circuit chip. There are others who contributed and obviously continue to contribute.

They are the **Work Horses** of our species. The rest of us are pulled along by them. They have constructive minds and engineer change.

At the lower levels of the Progressive Order, some strive to improve the status quo by small but significant degrees. There is continual upgrading of products, processes, and services and thereby general wealth by steady progress. They produce a new smartphone, a new automobile, a new television monitor, a new book every few years. There are countless numbers of these players on our planet. They usually work in large teams. Let's call them engineers or technicians. They shuffle forwards.

They are the **Worker Bees** of our species. There are lots of them; they buzz and continually drive progress by supporting the higher tiers of the progressives.

Using a very rough ratio scale for the three types of Progressive Player described above, we can guess; One to One Million to One Billion within our planet Earth's inhabitants.

The main contribution of the Progressive Players towards progress is positive.

The Neutrals

Figure 42
Zero effect

The neutrals make up the vast majority of the human race. There characteristic is that they are users of whatever products and services are available. They are happy to use rather than develop and influence. They are neither positive contributors nor adverse inhibitors of the stuff that drives progress. They are an example of Newton's Third Law of Motion; *Action and Reaction are equal and opposite*. They are a *Zero-Sum Game.*

They are interested in usage and their experiences of that usage. It's value to them and how easy it is to use whatever is being used. They are, in manufacturing terms, the operatives of the process. Going back to the Stone Age, they chip out the letters and hieroglyphs on the stone tablets. They do not decide what those letters and symbols are. The Dark Ages' monastic scribes who produced manuscripts were the ones who wrote the text but did not determine the text. Bringing us back to today's Digital Information Age, computer engineers and programmers provide us with Internet information services. These services enable the transmission of that information to we users but do not decide its contents.

The Neutrals are the recipients of wisdom. They maintain the status quo as

they use the products, processes and services of an economy to keep the wealth ship afloat. They are neither positive nor negative contributors to progress, but they are an essential constituent part. They are the journeymen or women of progress. But if the quagmire of bureaucracy slows them down, they do not produce growth. They are the real engine of change. If they are not working efficiently, then the economy that they drive is not working effectively and efficiently. The Progressive Players' gains are wasted through the deeds of others, as we shall now discuss.

Figure 43 Wind resistance aka bureaucracy

The Luddites

When naming this type of player, it was tempting to invent and coin a new term that describes them in modern parlance. But, the word Luddite is so appropriate, and it has stood the test of time. It has itself progressed with time. We might observe that it is even more applicable today than it was when it originated.

To understand this type of player, we have to go back into history again. Not as far as the Stone Ages or the Dark Ages but England of the late 18th and early 19th century. Then the initial social effects of the Industrial Revolution were being encountered. The industrialised use of steam was driving progress. The Progressives were applying technology to mechanise the weaving process. Textile looms were displacing the cottage industry of handlooms[22]. This was a big jump. Many weavers from the lower classes were concerned about their present and future working processes and prospects. They banded together locally to make a positive stance against the power looms. A feeling that was so positive that in places, they took hammers and smashed the new equipment.

Figure 44 Smashing tool this

This destruction was supposedly started in 1779 by a young lad named Ned Ludd. Thereby the term Luddite is common even today. By some accounts, Ned was a fictional character and leader. It's not clear that he existed as a person, so that we can consider him a cyborg or an avatar or even a cartoon character in today's digital speak. The Luddites' purpose was to stop progress and preserve the old ways of working. It became a potent force but was defeated

---

[22] It's interesting to note that handlooms were also operated by feet.

when the powers-that-be, as then, decided enough was enough. They took drastic and forcible action to stop it in its tracks.

Some might consider the Green Movement a modern offshoot of and be in the Luddites' traditions. You can debate this as you will, but at least The Greens are open, like the Luddites, about their intentions. Some may see these intentions as being negative as regards progress. Some may see them as positive regarding a better lifestyle for all and our small planet.

Figure 45 Green with envy

Yes, the Luddites were, and as we shall see still are, an opposing force concerning progress, but they were also a prominent and evident force. They were openly negative. They smashed machinery, and they were partially destroyed by whipping and being shot by soldiers. Originally there were not many of them, but today their numbers are quite large in terms of a proportion of the human race. Today's Luddites openly oppose the use of new-fangled things, especially what we call technology. They are Openly Negative.

The Digital Icebergs

For us, this type of player is the most damning of all the player types. It was tempting to call this grouping The Bureaucrats directly, but that in itself would have been an oversimplification. So why the label The Icebergs? Or, to avoid confusion The Digital Icebergs. [23]

If you consider real icebergs, they have specific basic characteristics. Their numbers are plentiful in polar regions, and they sometimes wander from these regions to areas with warmer climates. They are break-offs from the glaciers of the colder climes. They have a lot more of their mass hidden below the waterline out of sight than that which is visible. They are harmless until you bump into one of them, usually by accident, or they bump into you.

The Digital Icebergs that we are discussing are mainly not visible. Their activities are negative concerning progress. Their modus operandi appears to be progressive, above the waterline. In practice, they make sure that the benefits of economic growth and the quality of life are negative and have a braking rather than an accelerating effect. Real icebergs typically shrink in size

---

[23] There was a temptation to term this group the Dicebergs but the formulation and use of a new word in the English language would have brought about an avalanche of negative bureaucratic activity by the very types that it describes.

and have a lifespan of around one year. Digital Icebergs naturally grow, and when you encounter their activities, it feels like they will never melt away.

Digital Icebergs rule, OK? Ok? ok? oK? and if not, OK, try answering the question again or call the Help Desk whose number you can find when you have responded to the question correctly. There may be a queue. No, let's be positive; there will be a queue.

Summary of this chapter.

In this chapter, we have introduced the four types of progress players.

Some types have positive effects on progress.

Some do not affect progress.

Some have open negative effects.

Some have hidden negative effects.

This last type, The Digital Icebergs, encompasses modern bureaucrats who are using or misusing IT for their negative aims. Their arch-enemy is real progress. They live and work, often working hard, amongst us. Their influences can counter any gains from the real progressives.

10.   The dark art of bureaucracy

Abstract

Now, we begin to discuss, with some venom, how bureaucracy has lampooned the capabilities of IT, how it uses these capabilities to hinder progress. Thereby making sure that bureaucracy is up-to-date, state-of-the-art and automated. Bureaucrats are not Luddite Luddites; they move with the times and the technology of the times. They welcome new technology.

We introduce and define the terms of Progressive Bureaucracy and **Obstructive Bureaucracy.**

What is this thing, bureaucracy?

We've all got our mental model of what bureaucracy is to us. We have these models because we have encountered bureaucracy somehow in our lives, often irritating. Sometimes we experience it every day at work. Sometimes in our private lives.

As simple as possible and as complex as necessary – Albert Einstein

As made by Dr Einstein, the above statement was actually; *A scientific theory should be as simple as possible and as complex as necessary.* But we can extrapolate it to refer to *Doing something should be as simple as possible but as complex as necessary.* This is the mantra of our Digital Icebergs as we have defined them in Chapter 9. The types of Progress Players hate and have as their enemy. Defeating this is their raison-d'etre. Bureaucracy gets in the way of doing something. '*Something*' is often a process. Someone is going to do something, so let's get in the way and inhibit the doing.

Before we proceed, it's worth trying to understand that some types of bureaucracy are good, some types are bad. We often think that both types are *ugly.* They are not. The good is indeed good and makes a positive contribution to progress. We must have good bureaucracy, it is ordered, and we need essential order; else, we shall have chaos and inefficiencies.

What's the difference between good and bad?

Bureaucracy, the good form

Some consider that our world is naturally organised by its creator(s) or was. We reorganise it with our intelligence to make it better. Bureaucracy, in its good form, provides the organisation of the resources that will make positive progress. How much needed and what amount of help is needed for progress to happen is open to debate. Still, few would argue that we need zero organisation as a species and as nations or individuals.

This we can call Progressive Bureaucracy or Alpha Bureaucracy, **α** Bureaucracy.

Bureaucracy, the bad form

Some consider that our world is naturally disorganised. We need to reorganise it with our intelligence to make it better and smoother. Bureaucracy in its bad form attempts, and often succeeds, in stopping or slowing down progress.

This we can call **Obstructive Bureaucracy**, Beta Bureaucracy, **ß** bureaucracy and in this book, we often focus on this.

Obstructive Bureaucracy a definition

The term **Obstructive Bureaucracy** is *newish*. It was the writer Jerry Pournelle (1933 – 2017) who introduced the term the Obstructive Bureaucrat. He coined The Iron Law of Bureaucracy:

"...in any bureaucratic organization there will be two kinds of people: those who work to further the actual goals of the organization, and those who work for the organization itself... [In] all cases, the second type of person will always gain control of the organization, and will always write the rules under which the organization functions."[24]

For today though, we have moved the game forward. Forward from one played with a pen and paper to one played with IT. IT systems both of the business and commercial domains and personal domains.

Suppose we need a medical analogy for Obstructive Bureaucracy to give us a personal feel for its symptoms and effects. In that case, we can use the term Chronic Obstructive Pulmonary Disease (COPD). This condition restricts the breathing of a sufferer. Obstructive Beaurocracy impedes the progress of whatever it touches. It's worth attempting a specific definition.

Definition

Obstructive Bureaucracy restricts the efficient and essential flows of an organisation or an individual through excessive non-essential activities.

No definition is complete without a set of examples to illustrate it.

---

[24] Source https://tvtropes.org/pmwiki/pmwiki.php/Main/ObstructiveBureaucrat

Examples of Obstructive Bureaucracy

Let's investigate a few examples where **Obstructive Bureaucracy** degrades efficiency and often adds to the time of doing something. In the examples below, you will see a symbol ß in some places. This symbol is the Greek letter Beta which in English terminology is 'b'. In the vocabulary of this book, it is short for an instance and example of **Obstructive Bureaucracy.**

A symbol, in this case, ß, means just what I mean it to mean, said Humpty Dumpty. – Lewis Carroll (1832 to 1898) sort of from Through the Looking Glass.

What the world-famous egg said was, *"When I use a word"*, Humpty Dumpty said in rather a scornful tone, *"it means just what I choose it to mean – neither more nor less". "The question is,"* said Alice, *"whether you can make words mean so many different things?" "The question is"*, said Humpty Dumpty, *"which is to be the master, that's all".*

From this conversation, we can infer that the wonderfully famous Alice was a bureaucrat. The eventually damaged egg was a renowned fighter against bureaucracy before his demise.

Example 1 The walker

Let's now take the straightforward task of a walker going from A to B, where these two places are one kilometre apart. The walker is capable of walking at a steady 4 kilometres per hour. The journey can take several scenarios that might happen as:

1. When the walker reaches the point, A he or she sets out and walks to B, and it takes 15 minutes. The walker times this with his or her watch. This timing is an essential process and is α Bureaucracy. Without it, the walk is *timeless.*
2. When the walker reaches A, the starting point, he or she is asked to fill in a form to discover why he or she is walking from A to B. This form filling takes 5 minutes, and then the walker walks to B, where he or she is asked to fill in a form describing his or her walk experiences. This form filling takes another 5 minutes. The total time for the whole transit is now 25 minutes. 15 minutes of α Bureaucracy and 10 minutes of ß Bureaucracy.

In the first scenario, as above, the process is clean and efficient. The walker achieves his or her goal. No one knows why they made the walk or what they experienced on the walk. In the second scenario, there are two inputs of data sets. There is information output about *the why* and *the experience*. But the whole process took an extra 10 minutes. The information available doesn't add to the walking. It wasn't necessary for the execution of the walk. Question; was the additional 10 minutes of value?

The simple equation is:

Value of 10 Minutes of walker's time < = > Value of Information available.

Or simply; the effect of Obstructive ß bureaucracy = 10 minutes

The Digital Icebergs will maintain that the resulting Information is the dominant value. If they are challenged, they will then resort to IT to analyse the data in more depth and add the results to a volume of existing information. They have found a tool to retard the walker's progress rather than to speed up the walker.

Logic will get you from A to B. Imagination will take you everywhere – Albert Einstein

Example 2 The Driving License application

Let's take another example; this time, a little more complicated. A person wants to apply for a Driving License. There is a paper form to fill in. There is also an online form to fill in. The applicant goes online and gets the form displayed on a suitable end-user device. The applicant fills in the following data:

- Name, address, age, etc., all of which seems reasonable as a definition of the applicant. This is **α** Bureaucracy, and it's essential information.
- They then fill in Nationality, which seems reasonable, but it's not apparent why this is required. This is **ß** Bureaucracy.
- Then, he or she fills in Religion. It's not apparent why this is required and when the applicant answers, *Rather not say.* A new screen appears. This is **ß** Bureaucracy.
- This new screen requests why the applicant did not want to fill in their religion. This information does not appear on a driving license. The applicant is puzzled by now, and it has taken longer to make the application than expected. This is **ß** Bureaucracy. The applicant eventually gets back to the main screen and finds that this has timed out for security reasons. This is **ß** Bureaucracy.

- The applicant then starts again and eventually, through involuntary practising, gets the application finished longer than expected and with a higher frustration than expected.

There were four instances of Obstructive ß Bureaucracy in the above subprocesses of the above application.

The applicant has experienced that those who have specified the system have a desire to collect data and produce information. IT capabilities have enabled the Progressive α Bureaucracy, but it's easy to add an extra screen to the process. But the Digital Icebergs have added Obstructive ß Bureaucracy because they have lost a clear view of the essential function and have added branches to it.

Example 3 The hospital appointment applicant

This example is concerned with a person trying to get a hospital appointment in the UK. Inevitably this involves the UK's National Health Service (NHS). It is not the intention here to criticise a major and infinitely valuable institution that continuously makes progress toward better medical processes. But this is a real-life example.

- A lady receives a letter asking her to book an appointment at one of two hospitals. The letter has the telephone number and the digital address of the online appointment site.
- On several days she calls the appointment number on her letter but is always in a queue waiting for service. So she decides to try the online option.
- She logs-in with her reference numbers and is asked to decide which of the two hospitals she would like to receive her treatment. This is α Bureaucracy.
- First, she chooses the preferred hospital and clicks on that. She is informed: There are no appointments available. We can assume that this is α Bureaucracy.
- So she then clicks on the second hospital and is told: There are no appointments available. We can assume that this is essential and α Bureaucracy.
- She is now disappointed and a little confused, asking what she should do next. On inspection of the output screen well hidden from prominent view, *press here if you have not been successful in making an*

appointment. (It seemed that everyone trying to make an appointment would have to take this path!). The press was executed. This is ß Bureaucracy.

- On the screen came an instruction that asked the user to input their telephone number and email address in free text format. It told the user that they would be called or emailed to select an appointment place and time. This **is ß** Bureaucracy.

There were, and probably still are, lots of ways in which the user was subjected to bureaucratic delay.

- Why wasn't the user told that no appointments existed at either hospital when she logged in? This is ß Bureaucracy. Time was wasted.
- Why wasn't didn't *the call me or email box* come up straight away and be obvious? This is ß Bureaucracy.
- Why were the phone number and email address in free format text with all the chance for a mistake? This **is ß** Bureaucracy.
- Behind the scenes, someone now has to call or email the applicant in old-style efficiency. This is ß Bureaucracy.
- Why was the whole process so frustrating and took so long? OK, this was for only one person, but if you then multiply this by 100 persons trying to make an appointment, you quickly begin to see the effects on national productivity. This is Obstructive ß Bureaucracy. The outcome of the appointment application is not known. The frustration is known.

Example 4 Various shovels

There's an old story that goes something like this.

The scene is set in Victorian times in the UK. The setting is that of a cutting being dug for a railway line. In the cutting is a steam-driven excavator/shovel. At the top of the cutting are stood an industrialist and an early labour union leader. The latter says to the former; if it wasn't for that excavator, we could have 100 workers with picks and shovels working down there: the former replies, or 1000 with egg spoons.

Figure 46
Shove over

The productivity gained by using the excavator is evident. Still, if the bureaucrats are let loose on the new way of working, they can tip the scales back in favour of the men with shovels. How?

- The excavator is capable of moving 10 of its large buckets of soil per hours. A move takes 6 moves minutes. This rate represents the productivity of the excavator.
- The bureaucrats decide that the excavator is 10% more efficient each time it digs up a soil load with a clean bucket. They request that the bucket of the excavator is cleaned after each operation of the bucket. This task at a first approximation will increase the excavator's productivity to 11 moves per hour. A movement takes 5.45 minutes. This is seemingly real progress and growth. α
- But the cleaning takes 3 workers 5 minutes each time. These additional tasks mean that each move will now take 5.45 + 5 = 10.45 minutes. The excavator's productivity is now 5.74 moves per minute. Plus, you have to have 3 extra workers in the process. ß
- The workers with individual shovels have made a sort of comeback. So have, in theory, those with egg spoons. But as time progresses from the Victorian era, the efficient of excavators is improved. Eventually, smart excavators emerge. They do not need an operative or the workers to clean their buckets as they have self-cleaning buckets.

Improved technology efficiencies should mean that big engineering projects should be measured in a few years and the ordinary person's costs are understandable in the street or on the Internet. But no! ß

Example 5 The old ways go away
Sometimes the bureaucracy inherent in an IT system, perhaps even the system itself, spreads and influences *the old way of doing things*. The new system disturbs the ageing processes. What follows is a light-hearted example of this. Many will recognise the symptoms. Hopefully, it will be available on the Internet for many years though it could be replaced by something new!

https://www.bbc.co.uk/programmes/p083mv25

Example 5 Taking a holiday
While this book was being written, the pandemic labelled as Covid-19 struck the world. There were reactions of various kinds all over the world. In the UK, those in government recognised that people would have to isolate. Non-essential work would have to stop to limit human connectivity and, in particular, travel. Further, it was realised that this would cause financial hardships for many workers. So, the UK government introduced a scheme to alleviate this. The system was known as The Furlough Scheme. Workers could

ask the government for support while their employment was temporally suspended. It sounded good, but how many people knew what the word *Furlough* meant or even now means?

Figure 47 What does this mean?

The word could be looked-up in a dictionary, if you had one, or on the Internet if you were digitally connected. Or, you could assume its meaning. It was not a common word in the everyday UK life of ordinary people. So, why did someone make a bureaucratic decision to use the word *Furlough?* Why not use the word Markup or Topup or Makeup? Someone who was educated and highly literate added a hint of complicated bureaucracy to something simple. The measure of that added bureaucracy was that some had to consult a dictionary. Others had to spend time consulting the Internet, some had to ask others, some became confused, and some didn't understand and try. This was a prime example of **Bureaucratic Obstruction**. The **Clutteridge** added was the word furlough.

The intent purposely or accidentally was to be smart and get in the way of our end-users, maybe not to block them, but at least to slow them up and delay them. This retardation was probably not done on purpose (remember the Luddite category). It was done without considering the effects of using a word that was not in common daily-speak. The Digital Icebergs had struck without appearing above the waterline.

Example 6 Ivy and trees

Ivy (genus Hedera helix) is a common and somewhat pleasant plant. It grows around trees and supports many forms of wildlife. But the tree supports it.

There is a debate that whether ivy does or does not destroy the very tree which is its home or is it just part of the tree's environment supporting wildlife.

Do we have ???

or

Figure 48 I'm chipper?

Figure 49 I'm doomed?

Bureaucracy is like the question above. It often starts life as an innocent function, then it grows and clings to that function, and then the debate begins as to whether it is bad or good.

Example 7 The not obvious

Fighting resolutely against Covid-19, the UK government and the NHS surprised many with speed off the mark of the vaccination programme and then into the main task of jabbing everyone. After analysis, it was decided that the order of vaccination should start with the most vulnerable. This included the age group of 70 plus. They were either informed of their local medical practice slot or could book a slot on the Internet.

Many in that age group are not Internet savvy. But they tried and thought that they had booked their place and time. Alas, a screen showed that their choice had been accepted. But, to exact the booking, you had to page down the screen to close-off the transaction. The screen may have been a smartphone screen. Quite a few did not notice this. Quite a few turned up at the designated place at the designated time, *unexpected*.

What had happened was a classic example of elite designers sitting at a state-of-the-art screen, assuming that all users would be savvy. All users could handle the added bureaucracy of flipping down a screen.

Further considerations

Just taking two major infrastructure projects in the UK is High Speed 2[25] (HS2) and the tunnel under Stonehenge's renowned site [26] in Wiltshire, UK. The timescales of each are potentially ages by any modern standard costs are beyond the national budgets of many smaller countries.

Such projects are outstanding examples of the continuous bureaucratic hindrance that affects large UK projects and many other so-called advanced nations. In the UK, the construction industry is 7% of the total economic output utilising 7% of the workforce. The growth rate is around 1.3%. In some years,

---

[25] A high-speed railway running from London to several cities in the north of the UK.
[26] There's no real information on how long it took the workers to build the Stonehenge Monument but it can't be anything like the time that the tunnel is taking. After all the workers only had to bring the stones from Wales and fashion them and erect them in Wiltshire.

it's negative. The blame is usually aimed at the economy, with little connection given to the fact that the industry in question is a sizeable part of the overall economy.

We have a classic instance of a significant part of the national economy utilising the latest advances, yet constrained by what we describe in this book as the Digital Icebergs and their dark ways. Many large projects have significant cost overruns. Time costs in such projects, so it's not surprising that as **Obstructive Bureaucracy** elongates timescales, costs rocket. Bureaucracy costs money.

The Covid-19 Pandemic

While this book was rambling and rumbling its way to publication, the Covid-19 Pandemic struck the world, as we have said. It turned out to be a considerable opportunity for both the good and the bad types of bureaucracy to come into their very own degrees of excellence or resistance. Mr Newton's Third Law of Motion, *action and reaction are equal and opposite,* was about to be tested again. It is almost mandatory that we give Covid-19 Bureaucracy a few paragraphs in this book. As of the year 2000, we made everything Millenium Compliant, so we now make this book Covid-19 compliant.

The good activities, the positives.

The UK's preparedness for a pandemic of the nature and size of Covid-19 was, to all intent and purposes, non-existent. For many years, the health service (NHS) recognised the flu epidemic threat, especially during the winter months. But the readiness of essential items like Personal Protection Equipment (facemasks and gloves) was deficient by miles.

Also lacking were plans to deal with a significant epidemic, report progress regarding the affected volumes, and spread infections.

But as time passed and the essential needs became apparent. The bureaucracy swung into positive action, placing orders. Supplies were delivered where they were needed. Facilities were enabled, even new pandemic hospitals appeared from nowhere. Processes were defined and operated to execute vital tasks within days rather than months.

Lockdown activities, or inactivities, were defined, not entirely, and support enabled ailing businesses and personnel were offered financial help.

The good often defeated the bad but not in all quarters.

The bad activities, our old friends, the digital icebergs

There were examples of how **Obstructive Bureaucracy** was carried into the pandemic or was developed to hinder efforts to contain the pandemic.

*Figure 50
After you,
no after
you.*

The majority of the UK maintains that the European Commission (EU) is an overly-bureaucratic administration that worships its own status and practices **Obstructive Bureaucracy** with excellence. Some might even designate it as a 'holy temple' of it. The EU has to get its 27 members (was 28) to agree and make a decision. We have discussed the challenges above. In theory, this is an example of democracy. In less radical theory, it's an example of weak democracy. In many ways, it's an example of bureaucracy because it's not clear who makes the decisions. So faced with instant decision-making that bureaucrats see as being more menacing than an overactive herd of Draculas, they have to slow things down if progress is swiftly made.

An example of this affected the EU and no doubt its citizens with the 2020 pandemic. This example came to light, having been hidden in the dark in early 2021. It was concerned with the supply of vaccines, or we might say the lack of vaccines' supply.

Several nations' brilliant microbiologists identified vaccines that could protect the populations so hard hit directly by infection and indirectly by the lockdown. There were several tasks in between these discoveries and the protection of the people. The challenge was a global but a mainly national one. The very word *national* is imprecise if you are a national in the EU. The tasks were:

- Order adequate supplies from the vaccine manufacturers.
- Safely approve the vaccines for deployment – jab into arms.
- Get hold of the necessary doses of the vaccines, these having been ordered swiftly.
- Organise them to the designated persons by groups based on the supply that was inevitably constrained.
- Jab the arms and report the roll-out's numbers.

The UK and others like Israel and the USA set about the tasks above with what seems to be optimised efficiency. This surprised many in the UK but showed how those with the will could ignore bureaucracy to achieve a goal. The EU, on the other hand, or perhaps arm, was torn between centralisation and distributed control of the tasks. So the bureaucrats had an open field on which they could play their games. The results of the various contests were then precise for all to see. The crowds of spectators could see remotely even though they were not at the game.

The UK roared away, getting supplies and getting vaccination centres set-up

Figure 52
Liftoff

and getting the highest vulnerable groups vaccinated. The EU stumbled in approving the vaccines citing. They cited safety, and though an essential aspect, it's always an excellent bureaucratic delaying tactic. Orders were not swiftly placed, and populations began to wonder what was happening? The politicians and bureaucrats began to lay a smokescreen just as naval destroyers used

Figure 51
Steady as
she goes

to in a sea battle in the last century. In those days, thick smoke obscured the enemy. In these electronic days, it is useless and, of

course, not green. The fingers of blame were pointed at the vaccine manufactures, some of UK origin, for not allowing enough supply to the EU. That's what happens when the watchwords are; *anywhere but here.* Some politicians even muttered the threat of legal action against the UK and associated suppliers. We can but only imagine the result.

A prominent international court case ensues and takes six years to conclude. Some 98 microbiology experts give witness, some 43 contract lawyers give witness, and one German Shepherd dog gives witness because of a bureaucratic misunderstanding. The verdict is a retrial because of the complexity of the evidence. As portrayed here, such an affair is what might happen when bureaucracy takes hold, politicians get involved, and the legal profession takes up the baton.

Conclusions from this chapter

Figure 53
Not straight

There are two forms of bureaucracy at the highest level of consideration: the good form and the bad form[27]. The bad form we have termed **Obstructive Bureaucracy**. It is easy to spot but often hidden within essential processes and adds to the extras, meaning that the end-user has to take extra time and effort to deal with it.

Many large projects seem endless with continual meetings and reviews. They are never free of **Obstructive Bureaucracy** and thereby are never free of cost overruns and negative benefits. In general, the bigger the agency involved, the

---

[27] The use of the word *form* is not intended to be a bureaucraticly inspired pun but probably is.

greater the bureaucracy's effects and the less the progress. It's a long and winding road to completion with all sorts of extra turns and uphill stretches.

11. Productivity briefly explained

Abstract

The productivity of people writing learn-ed articles and books about productivity is astounding, so there is a lot to read elsewhere on the subject. But in this chapter, we effectively, hopefully, and with increasing efficiency, outline a view of productivity not just for physical products that are manufactured but for services and then for outputs of artistic people. These latter outputs seem to have been subjected to a drastic decline in their productivity. Perhaps this decline gives us some insight into why the real productivity gains of other forms of production are sometimes so small. We worship progress at the same time as worshipping falls in productivity. It's a strange old world that we live in.

At the beginning

When we started this rambling tome, there was a statement of concern that for the UK's and other such advanced nations, the economic growth rate is consistently meagre. By inference, this means that real productivity is near to flat year on year. Resulting from this is the lost opportunity of increased wealth for the nation as a whole and its citizens. It's interesting to ask; *the productivity of what?* In the context of our discussions, we can ask questions about the influence, positive or negative, as to the use of IT. At this point in those discussions, we can try to put some simple shape to the *what*.

We can classify the aforementioned *what* into three base classes:

1. Physical units of products
2. Services
3. Creative artistic works

You can invent more, but at this juncture, three is a manageable number. More would certainly be a sign of bureaucracy.

Physical units of production and products.

This classification is pretty easy to understand and measure. The products might be cars, textiles, beer, houses, books and a long list more. You can count their numbers quarter on quarter and see how these have grown or shrunk. In the chapter Types of Players, we introduced a player categorisation called The Progressives. We said that this was like a pyramid as regards its occupants. One of the occupants at the top of the

Figure 55 The hand that guides

Figure 54 Elites at the top

structure is the Scottish economist Adam Smith (1723 to 1790). In his brilliant and seminal work The Wealth of Nations (1776), he uses the pin's simple object to illustrate production rates. His wisdom is just as applicable today to the production of smartphones, nuclear power stations and pins. He introduced the concept of *the hidden hand* that influenced markets beyond that of regulation. We have *hidden activities* that affect and influence nations and businesses beyond statute and law. In short, that which is essential. Perhaps in honour of the man who many consider is the father of economists, we could say that bureaucracy and particularly **Obstructive Bureaucracy** is the *unseen trampling foot of progress.*

Services

Throughout history, services have been a part of civilisation's march towards economic progress and a better life. We can think of services as work and the performance of tasks or a set of tasks. The tasks might be commercial, military, artistic, or personal. They are usually done by one party for another party, often for a fee.

Today, services seem to be becoming a dominant part of a modern economy. Financial services, entertainment services, IT services, medical services, hospitality services, and public (government) services, to name a few. The list is extensive and seems to grow as, over time, all sorts of new services have

become part of the bigger economy. The magnetism of manufacturing with its factories drew 'the masses' from fields and cottages to factories in the Steam Industrial Revolution. Over the 20th century and into the 21st, the concentration points of services (aka offices) often drew 'the masses' from manufacturing centres. One of the essential components of bureaucracy is being pulled together; skills, especially IT skills.

Figure 56 The main attraction

Somewhat ironically, there is resettlement away from the office concentrations of skills. Workers are adopting the home working style enabled by the ubiquitous IT capabilities discussed in a previous chapter. It's a sort of *back to the cottages movement,* and it could well swing back more due to social factors. The aforementioned *from the cottages movement* of the first revolution produced social overcrowding in the towns and cities. The reverse direction, as with *working at home,* is often considered to create social isolation.

Creative artistic works

Consider these to be anything that we think of as artistic. Paintings, music, literature, films, performances, etc. The great examples of these are the top echelons' outputs of what we have described as the Progressive Pyramid. These outputs are often timeless in their appeal, and they form the foundations of the civilisations.

At first, it doesn't seem evident that the Digital Iceberg ones will hinder the Progressive Ones, but they can be. Let's investigate the productivity of writers and musicians over time. We'll take two examples of each of these; William Shakespeare (1564 to 1616, 52 years) and Tom Stoppard (1937, 83 years and going as at 2020) for the writers and Wolfgang Amadeus Mozart (1756 to 1791, 35 years) Andrew Lloyd Webber (1948, 72 and going as at 2020) for the musicians)[28].

Here, we shall not discuss the quality of the works of the persons in question. That is something for anyone to do as a lifetime's pastime or even a career. Neither do we discuss the length of a particular work when performed, how many times it has been performed, or whether it was for the stage, religious place, or radio/television.

Let us compare the output of top tier players of different ages. We'll start with writers and then move on to musicians.

Please note that none of these comparisons is intended to imply that any modern person is, to put it simply, trying, working or concentrating hard. The objective is to indicate that the modern environment in which they work is restrictive and holding them back.

Comparison 1 Shakespeare versus Stoppard

For this comparison, we'll use their output as playwrights of plays.

- Number of plays by Shakespeare: 40 (that we know of today)
- Number of plays by Stoppard: 30 (as of today)

It seems that WS was 33% more productive than TS is today, even if we ignore Shakespeare's other output like poems. Why is this when TS has all the technology/technical support of our age and WS had the paper of his time, a

---

[28] aka Baron Lloyd-Weber

quill pen and ink? Could it be that the bureaucracy of our modern era hinders TS's writing and its performance? Interesting?

Comparison 2 Mozart versus Lloyd Webber

We'll use their outputs as composers of today's classic operas and stage musicals for this comparison. Each composer may not have written the words to these operas.

- Number of operas by WAM: 22^{29} (that we know of today)
- Number of 'operas' by ALW: 21 (as of today)

Even allowing for Andrew Lloyd Webber's continuing output, he is no more productive with 'operas' than Mozart. His production per year of age is less than half of that of Mozart. Add to that Mozart's additional works of 41 symphonies, 15 masses, 23 concertos for piano and orchestra. Compare this to Andrew Lloyd Webber's additionals to date; 2 film scores, one requiem, 1 Variation for cello and you see an imbalance. Interesting?

Mozart would have had at his disposal the same writing tools as did Shakespeare. Stoppard and Lloyd Webber will have had for at least half of their productive lives the fabulous IT capabilities that we have today. At the face of it, we have a David versus Goliath match-up. Or a quill pen versus the laptop connected to the Internet. Which is mightier?

What we see with the two comparative examples isn't that one of the top tier progressives was more energetic of focused than the other. Today, we see that with all the progress that we have had with the technologies we have developed, progress has been surrounded by muted (sound off) bureaucracy for the modern playwrights and muffled (pianissimo-ed) for the contemporary musicians. Under the cloak of better organisation, the Digital Icebergs are winning. Technology is being used negatively. The Digital Icebergs use more technology and better effect than the Progressive geniuses purported to support.

Other musical examples are possible.

For the musical example above, we could have chosen Johann Sebastian Bach (1685 to 1750, age 65) and compared him to Richard Rogers (1902 to 1979, 77 years) or Lennon (1940 to 1980, 40 years) and McCartney (1942, age 78 and still going in 2020)

---

[29] 10 as a teenager

Bach wrote something like 70 organ works in a two-part form, an initial movement and a fugue. Some of these may not have been Bach originals, but there are undoubtedly many, and there may have been more. He wrote many more musical orchestral and choral works.

Richard Rogers wrote 22 musicals, Lennon and McCartney wrote almost 200 songs. Each Richard Rogers musical featured quite a few songs. But his output and the output of Lennon and McCartney do not match JS Bach's. When you consider the writing technology available to Bach and even when the others were writing, new technologies were available, perhaps not up to present-day standards. However, but they were better than a quill pen and paper.

We could also consider Cole Porter (1891 to 1964, 73 years). He wrote over 30 stage and film musicals without a lot of technical assistance. We could even attempt to compare painters and sculptures of the 15th century with those of the 20th century. The comparisons would be somewhat skewed by the size of the paintings that say Michelangelo (1475 to 1564, 89 years) sometimes did like the Sistene Chapel at the Vatican in Rome or the Last Supper (4.6m by 8.8m). These were on what we can describe as a 'big canvas'. Franz Joseph Haydn (1732 to 1809, 77) wrote 107 symphonies plus 26 operas and 14 masses.

Beethoven (1770 to 1827), on a single night in 1808, delivered three original works of his art: Fourth Piano Concerto, Fifth Symphony, Sixth Symphony. They have all survived.

These comparisons tell us something about productivity and progress that is hard to explain other than in the stark terms of that today's greats being retarded by what we are calling bureaucracy.

Scientific comparisons are possible

Compare the output of Sir Issac Newton, often mentioned in any scientific

Figure 57 I help concentration in 2 ways

context, with the production of any of today's leading scientists. Sir Issac's work was fundamental and thereby deep across several scientific disciplines and, therefore, broad. Fields such as the likes of motion, gravity, light transmission, cooling. Compare that with some of today's brilliant scientists, and you often see that they have spent a lifetime down an ever decreasing path of investigations. They are funnelled. Newton was T shaped and didn't have a laptop. Today we have I shaped geniuses who probably have many laptops.

What do we expect, and what can we conclude?

An expectation

Before we discuss any conclusions from the examples above, it is worth stepping back and asking; what might we expect to be the difference in the production of the types of experts we have compared? Start with an open mind. Imagine that you have newly arrived on Earth. You are part of a Martian mission to make a TV document. A documentary about the progress of civilisations on Earth and the accumulation of knowledge, and humankind's ability to progress continuously to a higher state of real knowledge.

We would expect that the 20th and 21st centuries experts should have been far more productive than those of the 16th to the 19th centuries. Why? Because of the following:

- The current experts have the foundations of the so-called 'old masters' to build upon by virtually standing on their shoulders, as Sir Isaac remarked.
- The current experts have an extraordinary amount of technology to aid them. This technology evolved rapidly in the second half of the 20th century. It was driven especially rapidly as the microchip and connectivity grew.

The report to Mars HQ, using advanced technology, concludes that writers, musicians, and artists have the environment on Earth to produce works and products at a better rate than their predecessors. But they don't seem to.

The reality seems to be different. We can say some of the factors that mean that Andrew Lloyd Webber isn't as productive as Wolfgang Amadeus Mozart. Tom Stoppard isn't as wordy-in-total as William Shakespeare? We can begin a list of possible differences as:

Figure 58 The bell is not chiming

- In olden times the greats were indentured to the nobles like The Duke of This or The Big Cheese of That. Every week they had to produce something for their employers like a Tocatta and Fugue or a picture.

- In olden times the greats were often impoverished and were paid pittances for their sublime outputs. Today, after a meagre start, modern greats are more than comfortable because of their early rewards.
- The olden-greats were unincumbered. They were so focused as to blank-out and ignored those around them who wanted to 'improve' their outputs. Added to that, communication in olden times was minimal. Today it is not limited; it is limitless.

It's that last entry above that leads us to the conclusion below.

A conclusion

A theme, perhaps even the theme, of this book is that something is getting in the way of progress. Real progress should be coming from the technology revolution that we are experiencing today. That something is what we call bureaucracy, as practised by what we have called The Digital Icebergs.

The fictional visitor from Mars will quickly spot the environments in which today's great progressives work have a fundamental design facet. That facet is the ability of the environment to ensnare progress. To bring about an apparent order in which the order is more important than the outputs of the processes it governs. Much of the inherent capability of our IT age is utilised towards this negative goal. In football and soccer terms, it's an own goal.

Conclusion of this chapter

This conclusion is short. Its main message is that the productivity of the great movers and shakers of our age is being throttled back by our age's bureaucrats. The population of Mars can see this. We, here on Earth, often cannot, and if we do see it, we don't do much to eradicate it.

Perhaps we need to go to Mars, come back to Earth and report back to Mars in triplicate?

12.   A spotter's guide to bureaucratic systems.

Abstract

This chapter looks at how bureaucracy can be identified and recognised for what it is and how it retards real productivity. There is a fixation on how the capabilities of IT are being harnessed to retard real progress. The Digital Icebergs, as we have called them, have realised the potential of IT to do this.

The types of systems that can be spotted as regards their origins and owners are identified. The reach of these systems considering the user communities is discussed.

In Chapter 10, The dark art of bureaucracy, we looked at some examples of how bureaucracy manifests itself. Now we look broader at where its sources are.

The Ins and Outs of bureaucracy

It's important to realise that bureaucracy wastes time the time of users of systems. It does so in two directions, these directions being during input activities and output activities.

Bureaucracy wastes an end-user's time when he or she inputs something either as text, touch or verbally. Extra unnecessary actions have to be performed, and frustration creeps in. As a

Figure 59 I shall say general rule;
this only once

The more you have to input to a process, especially in a free format, the more errors you make, The more mistakes you have to correct with new actions.

Correcting errors consumes time. When unnecessary time is consumed, efficiency drops. It all adds up negatively.

Bureaucracy wastes an end-user's time when they get output and have to ingest more information than is necessary to inform them of

Figure 60
More than what they want or should know. Sometimes necessary signals are
you need missed as a deluge of data is streamed at the end-user. He or she has to page through 20 screens when two screens would have been sufficient and efficient. Extra screens mean extra time spent.

Sources to be spotted and relished.

We can consider four types of sources where the bureaucratic wasting of time can occur. They are:

1. Governmental systems
2. Internal business systems
3. External business systems
4. Personal systems

Governmental systems

Previously, we used the UK as an example of a slow economic growth nation, so it's appropriate to consider some of the UK's national systems. Here is not the place to list those systems and comment upon them other than to make a very pertinent point about their influence on economic growth. That point is simply described as *extensive.* Governmental systems come in various forms:

- National
- County/State/Provincial
- Local community

The whole nation uses some Governmental systems. So if they are overly bureaucratic, they have a considerable gearing effect on the UK's efficiency because of the significant numbers factor. The number is potentially an adult population of some 63 million people who might use them. An extra screen or question requiring an answer here or there will mean vast numbers of hours wasted. There is added bureaucracy in collecting marginal data to produce marginal information. Thereby there is a substantial adverse effect on real progress. In this context, *marginal* is meant to mean *little positive value in terms of improvement and national wealth creation.*

True, not everyone uses the online Passport Application System every day. Still, the extra effort multiplies up when they make the extra effort. There's an interesting piece of bureaucracy in the UK passport application process. When applying, you must:

- Send the original documents. Photocopies are not accepted.
- If you do not have your original certificates (for example, your birth certificate), you need to get an official copy.

The above is a classic example of the confusion that can be caused by bureaucracy. The confusion is caused by misunderstanding (purposefully or accidentally?) the original and a copy of the original copy. If the original document is lost, how can a copy be made? What they are asking for is a duplicate secondary. The applicant probably never had the original, definitive birth certificate. The authorities did. He or she had an original copy. If, as the reader, you are now confused, you have been bureaucratised[30].

The message to any government in charge is simple. If you want to increase national economic growth, ensure that the bureaucracy in governmental systems is minimal.

The REACH of such systems is often **Nation-wide.**

Internal business systems

These are the IT systems that a private business or private establishment has deployed to run its business processes. In general, they are within the business domain and at the user interfaces of their inputs and outputs are the direct or indirect employees of the business. Typically employees are trained in these systems since these systems execute the IT aspects of the businesses processes.

If such systems are inefficient and overly fussy, then the productivity of the business will suffer. If data is not captured correctly at the input interfaces, exact information will not appear at the output interface.

An interesting example from a medical establishment that the author heard was; *we capture a lot of data and adequately store only about 50% of it. We analyse only about 10%.* The slack is bureaucracy by any definition.

The REACH of these systems is **Business-wide or Establishment-wide**

External business systems

These are the systems that private businesses open-up to the public to drive the business's processes with the end-users outside the company staff. This usage is enabled not only by IT online systems but by Call Centre Systems. Examples of these systems are:

- Online retail shopping – clothing, grocery
- Insurance quotations – house, automobile
- Travel bookings – rail tickets, holiday flights

---

[30] This is not a common word but it is a common effect.

Figure 61
Can I help?

- Fault reporting – telecoms connections, plumbing.

Businesses have been quick to recognise the potential of online systems that their customers can interface with for services. If they have not been rapid, then they have probably become ex-businesses. The advantages are evident, like getting the customer to execute the process and the execution time without the need for travel, to say the likes of a shop. Some sites appear to be *One-Stop Shopping*. You can purchase almost anything if you find it in amongst all the information presented to you. You get next day delivery if you are at home the next day.

The REACH of such systems is **Nation-wide or Market-wide**

Personal Systems

We might also call these Person to Person systems. We can, at the first level of analysis, classify them in two ways:

1. Email systems
2. Social systems

Both of these types of systems have grown dramatically in the last 20 years. Email systems, of course, replaced, to a certain degree, traditional mail systems. Not only in the person to person letter form but also the bulk email form. IT has made both forms easier, but it has made the bulk-email model much more manageable. Email is essentially a free service. Letter mail is not since stamps cost money.

Social systems, including Social Media systems, link together people of similar interests and sometimes localities. You can think of them as a set of electronic clubs. They promote social activities for good and sometimes bad reasons. They are voluntary because you have to join the club of your choice. You may not contribute, or you may be a significant contributor who it seems spends every hour of every day contributing to the contents of the information. Your input may be limited or extensive. The output that you receive can be overpowering.

The REACH of such systems is **Global.**

Bureaucracy by design

We will now consider how system designers, described above, can introduce bureaucracy into these systems, thereby inhibiting their effectiveness and efficiencies.

Extra data fields

When executing an online process, the end-user is requested to enter extra data. There is an input field to handle this request. The end-user does this but cannot understand why someone wanting to buy a bicycle tyre should be asked their age. Or why someone wanting an airline ticket from London to Edinburgh should be asked their nationality.

The data is being collected for other purposes than the mainline process.

The Key Question to spot this type of bureaucracy is:

Why *am I being asked to input this data?* **Why** *do they want it?* **What** *are they going to do with it in terms of storage and analysis?*

Extra process steps

As an end-user, you are happily filling-in an online form with the data requested. Suddenly you receive a message like; *Because you answered yes to Question 16, we are now going to ask you for some extra information about yourself.* (They ask you for additional data that they can turn into information, but the word knowledge is more attractive to some).

You are transported to the new step by a change of screen. You now have the task of inputting the additional data. You do this without understanding why you are doing this. At the end of this extra step, you search the current screen for the button to press to get back to the former screen. This button takes time to find, and eventually, the former screen appears.

The Key Question to spot this type of bureaucracy is:

Why *am I being asked to input this data on this extra screen/form?* **Why** *do they want it?* **What** *are they going to do with it in terms of storage and analysis?*

Complexity

The subject of something being involved and having complexity can be debated endlessly. Indeed complexity is a complex subject. There's a whole world of theory about it. Dictionaries define it in various forms, and one definition even equates being complicated to that of being tricky. In this sense, it means that doing something is a trick. Trickery is often the way that bureaucracy is seen by many of us.

Suppose we assume that complexity is in the eyes of the end-user. In that case, we can consider that the end-users of an IT system can be classified in three ways[31]:

1. Elite and expert end-users – can deal with any IT challenge
2. Coping end-users – can meet the IT challenge but struggle
3. Digitally Left Behind end-users – who are untrained in any IT activities.

The Elite end-users can deal with any complexity and probably enjoy its challenge. However, they may take more time than is necessary to deaden the effects than is necessary.

The Coping end-users get frustrated dealing with the overly-complex inputs and outputs of the system in question and usually get frustrated. Their efficiency is lowered.

The Digitally Left Behind end-users cannot use IT, and either do not use the system in question at all, or if they do, they ask a friend or relative to help them. This is sometimes a sub-optimal way of executing a process and sometimes isn't a reliable way.

Overall, the efficiency of those driving the process is less than it should be. Someone smart and probably an Elite IT person has designed complexity into the end-user interface. After all, they, or the team they are part of, want more than the end-users' minimum effort.

The Key Question to spot this type of bureaucracy is:

Why am I being asked to work out how to answers these questions? Why are the questions themselves so hard to understand? Do I need special training to answer this question? If the answer to that last question is Yes, then there is a big problem, and it's not with the end-user!

Options and the numbers game

Some end-user interfaces are made overly complicated and confusing by the sheer number of options presented to the end-user. The options numbers are much more significant than most people feel comfortable with encountering. Surveys collecting data for the quality of a product say are often like this. The end-user is presented with an input screen with ten rows and ten columns; thereby, there are 100 possible answers. In the table below:

---

[31] More about this classification can be found at http://bit.ly/IngeniaDLBC

Pn is the property of the product like say Quality, Value for Money, Durability

1 to 10 is the rating where 1 is Poor, and 10 is Excellent

	1	2	3	4	5	6	7	8	9	10
P1										
P2										
P3										
P4										
P5										
P6										
P7										
P8										
P9										
P10										

Figure 62 This is a Choice Example of Complexity

Figure 63 Merry square dance

The challenge to the end-user is obvious. The end-user isn't allowed to continue the survey until all columns have an entry and all the rows have an entry. The bureaucrats play the big numbers game to get comprehensive data to provide ample amounts of information. The value to the person who bought the product is debatable and certainly not direct in any way advantageous to them.

The Key Question to spot this type of bureaucracy is:

Who thought up these options? **Why** are there so many? **Is** a rating of 5 a lot less than a rating of 7? **What** are they going to do with it in terms of storage and analysis? **Shall** I ever see any results published?

Too much information and information overload

The human mind can absorb only so much information. Some human minds can absorb a lot more than others. Suppose we use the Elite/Coping/Left Behind categories as above. In that case, we can see a pyramid of the quantity of information you can throw at different minds. Many information systems tend to throw too much information out and let the end-user endure the excessive and work out what is important to them.

Systems overload maybe specifically designed-in to overload. Or they do so because they are not designed to filter output information. Sometimes this is a deliberate instance of bureaucracy. Sometimes, it is a side-effect of bureaucracy where the Digital Icebergs that we have often mentioned err on the side of overkill and overload rather than just right.

Emails are a real menace to busy people who have limited time to keep their mailbox down below umpteen gigabytes of information. For the average email user, there is a limited number of important emails. But there is a limitless number of ones to be deleted without any type of real inspection. The time taken even to delete the unwanted/unsolicited ones is wasted time.

Many emails and messages are themselves heavily overloaded with information. It seems that the following statement has been attributed to a legion of people whose lifetimes range from the ancient world almost to the Digital World. Still, it is as valid today, if not more accurate, than ever.

If I had more time I would have made this letter shorter[32]. Blaise Pascal, mathematician (1623 to 1662)

The long message is easily crafted using modern IT tools compared to paper, ink and quill pen. These IT tools are being used to waste time on the input phase of messages and more time on the output phase.

Another example of information overload and total bureaucracy can be found at sites that display a set of legal conditions and rules to the end-user. These are displayed to the end-user, and he or she has to flip endless pages to get to the button. At the bottom of the last page, there is a small box to tick. The tick indicates that the end-user has read the rules. The end-user is by then suffering from a deadened finger through excessive use of the page down key. They are left thinking, *has anyone who is not legally trained ever read all of this diatribe, and what's more, understood it?*.

Figure 64
Lawful?

The bureaucrats have had a field day or a court day.

Too little info

Sometimes the end-user becomes confused, trying to complete an IT task because the information a specific action in the activity will not complete, and

---

[32] What he actually wrote in 1675 was ; Je n'ai fait celle-ci plus longue que parce que je n'ai pas eu le loisir de la faire plus courte.

all that the user can detect is that there is something wrong with an input. The author was once faced with the following scenario when acting as an advisor in a local IT walk-in centre.

A lady comes in and has a problem filling with an application on her laptop. She has got stuck at a particular activity. After some trial and error, the digital roadblock is lifted and the action completed. Then the lady asks; *why isn't there a key on this computer that you can press, and it comes up with a list of actions you can do next to make progress?* The more you think about her problem, the more you begin to believe that she asks for something quite basic. Giving her guidance on how to proceed rather than waste time at a stop would give her real advice.

Figure 65
Locked out

Passwords are an essential part of IT systems at the end-user interface, so we are told. The consequences of not obeying the Password Rules are dire. There are no standards for the standards of passwords, so many use standard passwords. There are some conventions, but each site protected by a password entry system has its specified criteria. Quite often, when you are asked to create or change a password, you type in the new one, usually twice, to ensure that your entry is consistent. You get one of three happenings to occur.

1. The new password is accepted.
2. You are told that the passwords don't match but are not aware which one has your error in it. The end-user has to start all over again[33].
3. You are informed that your password does not meet the password standards of the site in question.
   a. It's a password that you have used before, and you are not told this.
   b. The password hasn't got enough characters in it, and you are not told this.
   c. The password doesn't have a capital letter, a number, or a *'special character'* or is a word from the dictionary, and you are not told this. What a *'special character'* is a special-secret.

---

1. [33] If anyone can suggest a solution to this dilemma and patent it riches are in store but anyone who has attempted to patent even the simplest idea is faced with more bureaucracy than they can imagine.

The bureaucrats are actively setting rules down that are sensible. Still, the end-users (aka customers) of their systems are not aware of those rules and must search for them before logging in or signing up.

The Jumblies

The Jumblies is a concept created by the nonsense poet Edward Lear (1812 to 1888).

Lear was one of those multi-gifted individuals who could write, paint and play music. What or who the Jumbles are in reality is a matter of debate, so part of their appeal is that they are unknown. We are often intrigued by the unknown and try to convert it to the known. Lear's poem The Jumblies doesn't define them. It only makes us think we know what they are. He's playing mind games with us. He's letting our imaginations run wild. Everyone who has read his no-nonsense nonsense poem almost certainly has a different image of what a Jumbly looks like or even sounds like.

Figure 66
Am I a
Jumbly?

He was a master of confusion like that. In his most famous nonsense poem The Owl and the Pussycat,[34] he uses the phrase 'they ate with a *runcible* spoon'. Almost every schoolchild who has ever come across this poem assumes well into adulthood that the word *runcible* has a meaning. Well, it doesn't, officially. In this poem, and in some of his other works, Lear makes us think that we know what something means and is, but we don't. But then we, the person, do know. He was, and remains, a master bureaucrat in that sense. For those who love his apparent stupidity, he's a good, if not excellent, bureaucrat.

In modern times we often hear the phrase; *what's going on here?* It's recently been used liberally in the book Radical Uncertainty by John Kay and Mervyn King. The term is self-explanatory and not at all confusing. But let's use it as an example of how bureaucracy can jumble up the words and cause confusion and waste time. We can shuffle away and play with the positions of words and ensure that the meaning of what we mean is not consistent like Lear does. The differences are a source of frustration. We can ask *What's going on here?*

Figure 67
How do I fit?

---

[34] See Appendix xxx for the poem. It's well worth a read.

> ➢ *Here, what's going on?*
> ➢ *What's going on here?*
> ➢ *What's here going on?*
> ➢ *Going on here, is what?*
> ➢ *Is what, going on here?*

This sort of reordering is the kind of nonsense, without poetic rhyme, that bureaucrats do with a simple and straightforward set of anything. If it's evident and straight forward, they can transpose it into something more complicated and confusing. A play on words is amusing when used in a comedy programme but wastes time when used seriously. The author is not joking about that.

At the start of this book, you may remember that poem transposed with the word *jealousy* being replaced by the phrase **Obstructive Bureaucracy**. It's that sort of trick that you have to spot.

Summary of this chapter

It is hoped that this summary is not too short and not too long. Too short, and it fails to make its key points. Too long, and it is by our definition overly-bureaucratic. The writer has fallen into a bureaucratic trap.

The right amount of information is essential, of course. The chapter is somewhat lengthy. It deals with how you spot the bureaucratic activities the Digital Icebergs build into IT systems. Where these extra activities are in end-user processes can be challenging to spot. The next chapter is concerned with why it is easy for these time-wasting activities to become part of IT systems these days.

13. How bureaucracy is practised

Abstract

As promised in the previous chapter, this is the next chapter. Having discussed examples of how bureaucracy infiltrates IT systems' end-user processes, we explore how IT has become a valuable tool. It has become an extension of bureaucracy and its obstruction of progress. We go back to the olden days to understand how bureaucracy has evolved and how significantly increased communication has made bureaucratic capabilities widely available.

Backs to the wall

In this case, the wall is the Roman Emperor Hadrian's Wall that runs across 73 miles of the North of England, where England borders Scotland. Or perhaps, it is the wall on which the writing was written in ancient times. So, we are back in

the days when a stone tablet or stone column was the media for information display and transfer. In those days, if the forerunner of today's Digital Iceberg, the Stone Iceberg, wanted to practise bureaucracy, she or he could ask the tablet chipper to add extra to the knowledge being chipped into the tablet. They might even ask for an extra tablet to be inscribed. As time passed, extra

Figure 68
Bureaucrats
worship here

parchments could also be recommended and even commanded if the inscriber was a slave. Extra anything is a sure way to increase bureaucracy and waste time.

The paper chase

As we come further through the ages, we find the same possible interference with data and information essentials. Paper becomes a common medium. The bureaucrats, the Paper Icebergs, continue to be limited by making their additions and extra add-ons that characterise bureaucracy. But the new medium of readily-available paper allows them to enlarge the subject matter and thereby waste the time of those who will read and absorb the outputs.

Suppose that as a bureaucrat, you were the scribe of an original document. You did have the superior capability to run riot with all the extras you could think up and pen into the work in question. But in general, interfering with production and progress was not easy and certainly not quick. Time to publish was your goal, no doubt, so those little extras had better be simple to insert. Otherwise, you, the bureaucrat, would be falling foul of bureaucracy yourself.

The arrival of the printing press was a boon to the production of information and repeated bureaucracy.

Communication enables.

As we have suggested in Chapter 9; The types of Progress Players, in past ages, you could only influence others' works if you were in the same place as them. If you were not, you could slowly communicate with them via a letter or perhaps a person carrying a message. The world was very different from that of today; it was primarily disconnected. Any connectivity was slow and sometimes not too sure. For example, to influence J S Bach, you would have to be in the same place or have an excellent letter service between you and the renowned organist if you wanted to tell him that you thought his next Fugue should not be in the key of G Minor.

As communications have advanced from written letters to telegrams, telexes, telephones, emails, emails with attachments, social chats, and live real-time videos, it has become easier for parties to join together. To communicate instantaneously, over any distance, with other individuals. It has become easier for those whose purpose is **bureaucratic obstruction** to practise their art, or is it a science?

Good communications become a channel by which bureaucracy can be practised and perfected. The better the communication channel in terms of

Figure 69
All wired up

endpoints and speed, the greater the effects on the output of real Progressives by Digital Icebergs. This impedance can happen within businesses and our society. It's sometimes called *Joined-Up.* You can have *Joined-Up Thinking,* which sounds excellent. Still, suppose it is so slow in producing a result. In that case, the result is probably out of date when it becomes real information that can make a difference.

Capabilities become ubiquitous.

One of the success factors that drove the automobile industry to such dizzy heights of production and acceptance is that most people with a little training can drive a car[35]. Most families with modest incomes can afford one or sometimes two vehicles. The user population is potentially everyone after a young age and before a great age. Thus it is for a car. But for an aeroplane for

---

[35] You can add the words *well and safely* yourself and debate their truth.

personal use, the skill to fly oneself safely is too great to master and the cost often too much.

At first, with even a pen and paper, not everyone could read and write. Nor did everyone have ample time to do so even if they could because most were often working long hours in cottages and factories six days per week. But *education for all* became the norm. So those that could read and write became the many rather than the few. Free time began to expand with shorter working hours and holiday time. The ranks of the potential bureaucrats swelled. Remembering our classification of players in Chapter 8, The types of Progress Players:

1. The Progressives.
2. The Neutrals.
3. The Luddites.
4. The Digital Icebergs

The Progressives, almost by definition, were always capable. Now those who we described as opposing players could become negative on a broad front. The Luddites' intension is to stop something from happening. There cause '*open*'. The Digital Icebergs' intension is also to stop things from happening, but their main objective is to slow everything down and make it harder to happen. They, with the name that we have given them, have hidden intentions. They are sneaky.

Figure 70 The other side of the fence

Early computer systems were the domain of very elite experts. To influence anything concerning their operations, you had to think, speak and write in strange ways called programming. There was a new set of languages to understand. Business managers could ask for *this, that and the other,* but this was in business-speak and not in computer-speak in a computer programming language. They could see outputs on listings and basic screens, as we have said. Still, they were in the hands, or more correctly, highly dependent on the elite experts' program sequences and dialogues.

As we described in Chapter 5, A short and narrow history of IT, the end-user scene exploded in all directions, particularly the directions of numbers of users and end-user capabilities. Quite suddenly, approaching and into the 21st century, virtually everyone had an end-user device of some sort. It was on their desk at work. Every home had a PC of some sort. Eventually, everyone had a tablet or smartphone on them and were connected wherever they were and are. Well, that's how it seemed.

The opportunities for the Digital Icebergs to practice their negative ways were everywhere and at almost any time. There were no real constraints in terms of logical or physical barriers or even cost limitations. It was in more basic terms like letting a group of young schoolchildren into a candy shop and letting them consume any of the shop contents without constraints.

Meetings and Decisions

Throughout history, decision making has been a practice ground for obstructive bureaucrats. Today it is a growing playpen for Digital Icebergs. They can use the ubiquitous connectivity intended for positive, productive activities for their negative, get-in-the-way actions. These actions are especially true in meetings, especially in remote sessions, since you often can't detect their body language.

When in doubt about a specific challenge, one of our human actions is to hold a meeting of interested parties. Undoubtedly, from the earliest days of tribal living, the elders would gather at some designated safe place and discuss and debate the solution to the moment's challenge. Nothing has changed over the centuries though now the safe domain is a conference room. The appearance of wolves is improbable, and a visit from members of a neighbouring tribe rare. At present, parties' meeting may be remote, and everyone is present by connection rather than physical presence. There is the possibility of partial or total blackout, and no one can be sure that the wires are untapped. A hostile business tribe is not listening. It's a bit like the elders of a tribe meeting in an enclosure and being unsure that enemies are not overhearing their deliberations. At least wolves did and still do, advertise the presence.

Figure 71
In doubt?
Hold a
meeting

To add particular importance to what is a meeting, you can call it *a round table discussion. A round table discussion* is an example of using four words instead of two (open bureaucracy). Of course, it has that perception of regal history and chivalry. It's a link back to King Arthur[36] and his knights of the fabled round table. It is as though a meeting around a rectangular table does not have the same appeal. It does

Figure 72
Gather round

---

[36] Late 5th Century to early 6th Century. Also known as Arthur Pendragon.

bring forward the question for those planning the meeting venue. How you fit a sizeable round table into a square meeting room? These days of remote sessions also bring forth the question of how you have *a round communication*.

Then as with any meeting, a decision has to be made. After all, that is the

*Figure 73
Undecided*

raison d'etre of meetings, unless you are of an obstructive and bureaucratic mindset, as we are about to discuss. A vital decision of any meeting is to decide how a decision gets made. Must it be a unanimous vote? Must it be a majority vote? Or must it be the likes of a 66% vote? Into what we can call *the void of non-decision,* the obstructive bureaucrat can advance.

We often see the obstructive numbers game being played, and the base logic goes like this.

- If there is one person who has to decide that one person has the unanimous vote but does have to collect all the facts and criteria.
- If ten persons have to make a unanimous decision, they have to be sure and make the decision. That may take more or less time than the single-person decision. Into such a decision tree these days, the Digital Iceberg can extend the whole process with phrases like:
    o Do we have the problem defined sufficiently?
    o I need more information.
    o I would like to see a deep dive into aspect 2.
    o Are we sure? Should we bring in a fresh pair of eyes?

    Indeed in this environment, the Obstructive Bureaucrat can wield great power and influence. She or he can run the show, set the pace and inhibit progress.

- Suppose ten persons have to make a majority decision. In that case, the Digital Icebergs will attempt to form their own sub-meeting. The objective being to muster the negatives and delay the decision making. Choice phrases can be heard:
    o Should we form a sub-committee to consider that aspect?
    o Let's employ external consultants?
    o What's China's reaction to this going to be? We need local thinking.
    o Is this safe and secure in our modern digital world?

    o Have we considered all the options?

Here we do not propose with any certainty that having more people make a decision is better than having one or two. But we comment that what modern digital facilities allow to those opposed to rapid progress is perpetuating meetings and elongating decision-making. They can form teams. This behaviour is **Obstructive Bureaucracy** at its finest.

One way of making sure that meetings will be held is to set up a committee. A committee is a commitment to hold meetings regularly. The record of each session can end with the choice phrase; *Date of next meeting.*

On the 17th of January 2021, the UK newspaper The Sunday Telegraph ran an article that reported that the UK Prime Minister had asked the UK's Chancellor of the Exchequer[37] to eradicate the Red Tape Legacy of the EU.

*Figure 74
Does anyone have a match?*

In doing so, the UK's bureaucracy would seemingly be reduced. This action, it states, will be done by forming a committee that will get to work on the task with what seems to be some urgency. To speed up the job at hand, it appears that more committees will be set up. If this is true, we can only fear that we will experience another classic example of how bureaucracy gets generated and perpetuated. We can, with a little imagination, anticipate the outcomes of these committees over the next few years with recommendations and dictates like:

- All red tape will be renamed blue tape and require Royal approval.
- All red tape will now be officially green tape to conform with carbon neutrality.
- All red tape will now be cut with a pair of officially approved Severance Scissors which can be obtained by filling in a form ScissorsPQ178-V1.2 on any government website.
- We'll replace this old EU regulation, which went to 92 pages, with a new law with 9 parts, 3 subsections, and 6 Appendices. There will also be a Code of Practice.

A key message is: Beware of those who want to destroy red tape with red tape.

---

[37] The one who owns the purse strings and in this day and age we assume to passwords to the national bank accounts

Quangos

In the UK, we have a set of 'Super Committees' that are known as Quangos. The word itself reeks of bureaucratic essence and a way of obstructing progress while consuming funds. Like with bureaucracy in general with quangos, there are good outcomes and bad outcomes. The whole subject of quangos comes under the gloriously emotive word of *quangoism,* which isn't formally defined, so it is exceptionally appropriate to the residents it covers.

Figure 75
We count
beans for
them

A quango is a semi-governmental body whose staff are not the regular national civil servants. The leaders are not part of the government, either the elected members or non-elected civil servants. But the leaders of the quangos have been appointed by the government and are, in theory, responsible for it. Quangos are often classed as *Arms Length Bodies (ALM's)* supposedly to signify their political status and social distancing from official government agencies. Herein lies a puzzle for the ordinary person in the street.

If faced with a national task, big or small, the government has the authority to decide, either by past experience or by a new decision, that it will insource the execution of the said task or it will outsource it. But quangos seem to be a halfway house in which the government keeps some control. We might even call this half-sourcing[38]. Control is maintained because it is the government that usually funds the activities of the quangos. The number of quangos in existence in early 2021 in the UK is a matter of debate. Some put the number at 300. Some at 400, and some even bend the definition to around 1200. Perhaps there needs to be a quango to control and number quangos?

Officially, as printed in the UK Government Document *Cabinet Office Public Bodies 20181-19 report*[39] as of 31st March 2018, there were

- 391 Public Bodies (aka Quangos to us) consisting of
  - 37 Executive Agencies
  - 242 Non-Departmental Public Bodies
  - 22 Non-ministerial Departments
  - All seem to have websites.

---

[38] Haldsourcing is a new word in this context but there is a website that is loosely related to it.

[39] Public Bodies 2018-19 (publishing.service.gov.uk). It's interesting to observe that this report was signed-off by The Minister for The Constitution. It may surprise some, perhaps many, that the UK has a Constitution. In fact it has what is called a Uncodified Constitution which we can interpret as a jumble of documents and not a specific document.

- 278,062 Staff
- Expenditure of £203.8 billion

There is an assertion that the number of quangos is falling. There is no doubt that there is a stream of political rhetoric that a bonfire should be made of them and ignited. Quango Bashing is a national UK Passtime. But to the average observer, quangos seem to be like one of those monsters encountered in Sci-Fi films. The 'goodie' cuts off a tentacle, and another tentacle grows. As one is 'retired', another one springs up with an obscure name, and therefore its purpose is likewise.

Figure 76 Ignite

As a very rough measure, their total budget was £205 billion per year (say 266 USD). The UK's Gross Domestic Product for 2021 is estimated at £2304 billion, so quangos are about 9% of this. Some contend that although the number of quangos is falling, their costs rise because of increased rump staffing. Whatever the real numbers are, the whole subject of quangos appears to be confused and inexact. In such circumstances, the potential for our chosen topic of bureaucracy to blossom in the good and the bad sense is considerable.

For those from outside the UK and perhaps 99% of UK residents, here is a selective list of quangos to illustrate their characters.

- The British Broadcasting Corporation (BBC)
  - A world-famous broadcaster with a budget of about £5 billion
  - About £3.5 billion of that comes from license fees, which is the most direct form of taxation that you can imagine.
  - Staffing is 22,000
- The National Health Service (NHS)
  - Much maligned as an organisation[40], much appreciated as a function
  - The UK Department of Health itself has 27 quangos.
  - The NHS is a colossal quango[41]
  - The NHS Budget for 2021/22 is £160.9 billion (this does not include special Covid-19 funding)[42]
  - Staffing of 1.3 million
- Office of Civil Society (OCS)

---

[40] Special note: The author's personal experiences of Primary Care General Practice Management and Hospital Trust Management is that both are excellent.
[41] Biggest anywhere by the definition of a quango.
[42] Source: King's Fund 11th December 2020.

- o Is part of the Department of Digital, Culture, Media and Sport (see below)
- o Is responsible for policy relating to young people, volunteers, charities, social enterprises and public service mutuals.
- o The Budget of OCS not clear.
- o About 100 staff.
- Office of the Immigration Services Commissioner (OISC)
  - o Is part of The Home Office
  - o Regulates immigration advisers, ensuring that they are fit, competent and act in their client's interests.
  - o The Budget of OISC not clear
  - o The staff of OISC not clear.
- The Department for Digital, Culture, Media and Sport[43]
  - o Has 2 non-ministerial departments
  - o Has 34 non-departmental public bodies
  - o An expenditure of £1,528,807
  - o Staffing of 13590

Before leaving this section, it is worth reflecting that much of the above discussion is concerned with quangos. They are, by definition, an attribute of the UK government and governance. Suppose the reader is not familiar with UK governance. In that case, she or he might want to reflect upon the quango-like bodies that are or are not part of their own country's government. There must be some because of the good bureaucracy needed. But there are probably some that constitute the harmful or Obstructive Bureaucracy that we focus on in this book.

Conclusions of this chapter

What we have seen recently is what we might call **IT Saturation**. Digital interfaces are with us all the time, sometimes even when we are sleeping. These interfaces are a fantastic platform for the Digital Icebergs to practice and slow down and expand simple activities. They make them so complicated as to make them ineffective regarding their efficiency and the efficiency of the end-users.

Suddenly, the audience for negative digital activities is global and not limited to theatre or cinema size. It is like The Glastonbury Music Festival being

---

[43] It's hard to spot a common factor in those four words.

streamed all over the world if you are a bureaucrat. You can perform on the global stage. Government departments can perform on the national stage. The audience that you can influence with your negative ways is limitless. One extra keystroke in an interface that is extensively used say answering *Yes* to an *Are you sure?* message can have untold productivity effects on our societies. The IT system costs of inserting an extra message are small. Because IT is on an excellent price-performance curve, the cost will continue to fall. But the cost of time for the end-users will rise. Time is money for many, especially when providing services, so as time is wasted, so is money.

The decision-making processes that are so essential for rapid progress can be elongated. Bureaucratic interference extends the meetings at which decisions are made. The Digital Icebergs can snugly think:

The digital world is my bureaucratic oyster.

14. How IT can be used as the engine that drives Bureaucracy

Abstract

We now investigate how some of our current IT systems' easy-to-use facilities help the Digital Icebergs execute their activities. Activities that slow down businesses' real productivity and private individuals with their excessive use of ordinary communications functions like emails. If you want to slow someone or something down, you send them a string of emails.

Bureaucracy is an add-on to normality, a sort of minus-on with red ribbons.

Excessive emails

We have discussed in a previous chapter, 11, the potential for emails to waste time. First, let us imagine we're inside a business where many of the workers are sat at workstations and have sign-on id's. Each can receive three types of emails:

1. Essential emails for a business process like an order from a customer for a product or service.
2. Information emails that provide information about the working environment like say achievements and personnel changes.
3. Time wasting emails that make the recipient wonder, *why has this been sent to me?* I'm spending time deleting it, let alone reading it.

Secondly, let us imagine that we are an individual with a personal email account. We can receive three types of emails that are not dissimilar to the sorts of emails above.

1. Essential emails that have important documents attached or pointed to like invoices and bank statements.
2. Information emails providing information about our declared interests like meetings of associations that we are members of or 'letters' from friends.
3. Time wasting emails that make the recipient wonder, *why has this been sent to me?* I'm spending time deleting it, let alone reading it.

In both of the 3 cases above, persons are wasting time. Their business or personal productivity is reduced through The Digital Icebergs' actions, who are responsible (or is it irresponsible?) for the emails. It's worth asking the very pointed question; *why do they do this, and how do they do this?*

The answer to that two-part question is; this is what the Digital Icebergs do, as we have said. They have available to them the same necessary IT facilities that are intended for productive use. They can construct an address list of any size and automatically send an email to all addresses in that list in what is an electronic flash.

Figure 77 Two-faced usage

We have just encountered an excellent example of a technical function's productive use being turned around into an unproductive use.

Excessive data in

As well as emails being a waster-of-time, we have also discussed earlier how excessive or extra data being asked for at the input stage of a transaction can waste time.

In this somewhat covert activity, the end-user is asked to fill in a field on a screen (a digital form, for instance). The end-user struggles to understand why they are being asked to provide this detailed data. It does not fit with the

Figure 78 Fill-in all fields

profile of what the end-user is doing. The demand for this extra data originates with someone thinking that it would be an ideal opportunity to collect this data from end-users. The end-users are executing an activity loosely coupled to the essential end-user process. They are captive, for instance, rather than asking the end-user to tick a box that says that they are over 18 years of age. The end-user is asked for their year of birth. To help or often hinder, a list of years suddenly appears, often including the current year. If the end-user is, let us say, over 80, they end up with fatigue getting to the appropriate year at the bottom of the list.

The question that can be asked is; *why has the extra input been added?* Once again, the answer is two-part. First, this is what the Digital Icebergs do, as we say again and again. Secondly, it is now easy to add extra input fields to a screen or sometimes even add an additional screen. In the old days, to add an additional field would have meant reprinting a form. Reprinting was a costly and slow process. But today, with screen editors, almost any coping person can add an input field to a screen form, and the resulting data can be stored,

Once again, we see the ease-of-use of an IT facility like a screen generating tool. It can be used to indent the productivity of the end-user.

Excessive information out

We are indeed in the Information Technology Age. If we wanted to be brief, we are in the Information Age. The technology is infrastructure by which and one which the information is manufactured and delivered as we have discussed in chapter 7 How information is manufactured, stored and distributed. In that chapter, we briefly discussed how an end-user gets both solicited (*I asked for it*) or unsolicited information (*I didn't ask for it*). Here we're going to consider the middle ground that we can describe with the phrase; *I asked for something like this but didn't expect this.*

One of the genuinely fantastic advances that we have seen in the IT age is data and information digitisation. Anyone with suitable connectivity can access the big data store. It's not just the extent of the stored data but how the data is indexed and structured so that with a few well-chosen keywords, the answer appears. Yes, the response does appear as though by glowing magic, but lots of other information appears as though by black magic. The search engine that has been used by the end-user, sometimes by choice and sometimes by default, has returned the answer or several answers. These are surrounded by all sorts of what we'll call padding answers, some of which are advertisements.

Taking a simple example; the end user types in *the square root of 2.* Back

comes a 1.41421, which is the answer but also comes back a pointer to what a square root is. This is OK. But also comes back information that people who looked for the square root of 2 also looked for the square root of 3. Then there may be a pointer to a site that tells you how to calculate a square root by hand and assuming brain. Then there could be a pointer to the pop group's website, whose name is Square Root[44] and a company called Square Root Group Limited[45].

Figure 79 Don't waste thyme or time

Here, someone has enabled the search engine to execute precise and fuzzy searches on the data and provided more examples of the hits than the originator expects. So there is a blizzard of information, most of which he or she doesn't want.

---

[44] BTW there doesn't appear to be one – yet.
[45] BTW There is one and there is no evidence that they are advertising in this way.

Over and over, we see that the very same IT that can give you the answer can be used to provide you with more solutions than you want. In dealing with this extra output, the end-user wastes time.

Conclusion of this chapter

IT is wonderful and beautiful. It is often an unbelievable part of human progress and intelligence.

Its benefits to business and individuals are legion. It can also be used as a tool to produce adverse bureaucracy that becomes what we are calling **Obstructive Bureaucracy.** This happens when those who employ and deploy it build-in excessive activities for end-users for inputs, outputs and process steps. The result is reduced efficiency all round.

15. Bureaucracy makes my eyes smart

Abstract

This chapter discusses the current vogue, *Smart,* which means that almost every new project and how to do things are labelled; Smart. How those who promote smart this, smart that, and smart the other have lampooned without the associated humour the real potential of today's IT. If it's smart, it's about IT and if it's about IT is has potential for induced bureaucracy.

Smart

What does smart mean? We can consider two meanings in two senses. There are more meanings and senses.

- The first being the meaning of smart in a dictionary sense.
- The second being the meaning of smart in a management and consultancy sense.

In the dictionary sense, smart has quite a few different meanings within different contexts. It's one of those words that is comparative as opposed to absolute.

- *He's smarter than him.*
- *She's not as smart as her.*
- *I wish I'd bought a smarter dog.*

Smart is not a physical value or measurement on a scale like a length or weight. The value of someone's IQ (Intelligence Quotient) can be used to grade a person's smartness. For many years, the subject being graded was, of course, a human being, or sometimes an animal. It could be said that something was a smart move, let us say to sell something when it was high priced, but the subject was a human being, or a group of humans, in the end.

In the management and consultancy sense, smart, as an acronym, was first described by George T. Doran in 1981 in his paper *There's a S.M.A.R.T Way to Write Management Goals and Objectives.* His terminology was:

1. Specific
2. Measurable
3. Assignable
4. Realistic
5. Time-related.

These are highly-desirable attributes of a management style but let's keep them in mind when discussing the Smart Revolution (as so-called) of today.

As engineering abilities improved and the Electrical Revolution got a grip, a piece of technology could be smart but was usually a mechanically enabled extra function. Real traditional engineers could, for instance, use electric motors to take manual activities out of process tasks. This practice was across a broad spectrum of applications from mega-engineering, say elevators in skyscraper buildings or whole manufacturing production lines, to domestic appliances like washing machines and personal hair dryers. The entire movement went under the general title of *automation,* and of course, it continues today. This automation enabled the new and took the manual out of the old.

The chip's power and capabilities drive the IT age forward at a dramatic increase and cost reduction rate. Chips begin to become part of a whole host of new products and are added to older products. This was a continuation of electrical automation as described above. But of course, the programmability of the chips made functional enhancements potentially much more significant. The whole idea seemed revolutionary and progressive. Then someone, perhaps everyone, suddenly began using the label smart for anything trendy.

Someone, somewhere, began to refer to the new automation style characterised by adding chips and programming to everything as Smart. The Smart Technology Revolution or Movement had begun.

Suddenly smart new labels were put on all sorts of entities like:

- Smart cities, whole cities.
- Smart motorways, trunk highways.
- Smartphones, phones with cameras, screens, internet connectivity.
- Smart home products, like doorbells, televisions, freezers.

This Smart Revolution isn't directly defined by either the dictionary or the management consultancy descriptions listed above. It's something new. It's a continuation of automation, and it is associated with chips and programming, but it is under the covers and marketing initiative that you can hang your hat on if you want to do something new. Alas, and returning painfully to the subject of bureaucracy, it is an ideal hat-hanger for those bureaucrats who wish to gain control over something. The something is now often inanimate.

Not so smart, somewhat dumb

Let us look at the list of the smart things above and see how the Digital Icebergs piggyback on these for hidden reasons of bureaucratic control.

Smart cities

One of the significant challenges of almost any city in the world is traffic. The problem's depth varies from city to city, but generally, there are often two rush hours at the beginning and end of each working day. If there is one rush hour, the problem is probably that the rush hour is that the rush hour lasts many hours. Somehow cities are reasonably organised to house people and provide places of work. Still, they are poorly organised for surface transport. So the Digital Icebergs descend upon the traffic challenge.

Figure 80 I'm on a charge

The smart city answer is to monitor the traffic flows and congestion with technology. To analyse this data to optimise the flows by analysing the real-time data that is forwarded to a central system and dynamically adjust traffic signals and the like. Such practice has reasonable goals and intentions. But, also technology allows an adverse bureaucracy to be practised. This is concerned with charging vehicle drivers for entry into areas of the city. Supposedly it should deter entry, but this isn't very certain. What it does do is set up processes that mean that the drivers have to pay, and if they don't, an organisation ensures that they do pay. We thereby have:

Smart traffic city = Benefits of optimisation – Overheads of charging

Suppose those who design the charging scheme want to. In that case, they can also charge larger or polluting vehicles extra to enter the city. Once again, technology is the Digital Icebergs' friend. They want to impose upon those who want to do something relatively simple.

Smart motorways

In the UK, the main arteries between and around the population conurbations

Figure 81 All systems slow

are call motorways (M1, M3, M8, M25 in the UK, for example). As a rule, these are dual three-lane highways. Plus, on each side, there is an extra lane for stopped vehicles that are in trouble. Many of these motorways, especially on specific stretches and at certain times become clogged. The answer was announced as a conversion to Smart Motorways. The end-users seemed pleased but were unsure of what this meant in practice.

After many, many months of sitting in extra traffic jams and enduring speed restrictions, the conversion works from Stupid-Motorway to Smart-Motorway eventually began to end. The output became evident. In sum, it was and is:

- ✓ The breakdown lane is now a full transit lane. Thereby the throughput of the highway is increased.
- ✓ There are many more signs providing information about what is ahead and, in particular, whether a lane, especially the former inside breakdown lane, is blocked.

Alas:

- ✗ The new signs' information is not real-time; thereby, if a lane is closed, drivers cannot immediately realise this.
- ✗ If a vehicle does breakdown and stop and the driver cannot get to a safe-haven, he or she has to stop on the new inside fast lane. The dangers are evident.
- ✗ Many more hidden speed detectors are installed to increase the potential for speeding offences with all associated bureaucracy like that of the City Charging Schemes.

Yes, the new motorways are Smart Motorways but are they smart? It seems that they are an excellent example of the practices of Digital Icebergs.

Smartphones

Smartphones are indeed a progressive step. New models appear regularly with new must-have features. But what is smart about them? In essence, they combine several products in a small structure and at a reasonable cost. They have a chip in them, well, more than one. They have combined a phone's functions and have mobility. They host an Internet browser and an email interface. They provide a camera and several administrative functions like a calendar, music player and an alarm clock. Yes, the design and packaging is very smart, but what is smart about the functions? The smartphone is a lot more desirable than a dumb mobile phone, but there are no breakthrough functions, as yet, on a smartphone. They are an amalgamation of functions. They are repackaging in one convenient bundle. When there are ingenious new functions, what will it be called? Smart smartphones, no doubt!

Smart home products

Our homes have been deluged with chips. These have entered as the components of our household products. These used to be basic engineered products to systems on their own or part of a connected network within the household or even the global system.

Many of the household products that we have today have regressed backwards on the automation trajectory. They have become so complicated that users have to unravel their complexity. Take, for example, an ordinary, as today, domestic clothes washing machine[46]. It has more control functionality than many commercial aeroplanes had 50 years ago. There are so many functions and sub-functions available to the end-user who is not offered the equivalent of pilot training. A few years ago, such training or familiarisation would have been accomplished by the age-old activity of *'Read the Manual'*. The modern appliance doesn't often have a paper manual (or a stone one for our historical perspective), but the end-user is asked to go to the Internet and inspect the manual on-line. When there is a problem, the user gets out a tablet or goes to a laptop and looks up the model's washing machine manual in question. Searches for the answer to his or her query. The problem is answered.

Figure 82 It's been washed eventually

The time spent getting the answer has been elongated because the questioner has had to use another product to obtain the solution[47]. The power of the chip and programming have together caused the end-user to have to spend more time than he or she could (aka bureaucracy) in the answering of a simple question due to:

1. The sheer complexity and diversity of the functions involved due to the use of the chips and programming.
2. The assumption that the Internet with all of its information is instantly at hand to someone wanting to use a washing machine.

The Digital Icebergs have had their way of designing or over designing a Smart Washing Machine. Automation as a means of saving time is going backwards and is a means of consuming time.

---

[46] The example that follows is not based on any particular washing machine but is an illustration of the type of situation that many users of many current smart products endure.
[47] Without doubt someone, somewhere is solving this problem by building a full Internet facility with an advanced browser into a washing machine to further complicate a basic task.

Conclusion of this chapter

Chips and their associated function are everywhere, and it is very fashionable to splatter them everywhere and label the resulting object as Smart as though it was a step change for humanity. Sometimes the change is progressive. But it can mean that the real end-users wonder if the smartness isn't a hindrance, rather than a real benefit when considering function and time spent to achieve something quite simple.

Chips are everywhere. Is this universally smart?

16.　　The dumb cost of bureaucracy

Abstract

Relax because this chapter is not loaded with shedloads of economic data and monetary values beyond a typical working person's comprehension. The Internet is loaded with such data and information. A lot of it conflicting when studied.

This chapter tries to build a picture of the lost opportunity that IT's proper and non-bureaucratic use can produce. The subject of regulation is introduced into the melting pot for discussion. Beware so is the subject of taxation, which is not one that most people view with satisfaction.

Some costs

In the best traditions of the contradictions in this book, having said that the will not be monetary figures in this chapter, we start with some.

Much earlier, we posed the question; *why does the UK have a low and meagre economic growth rate?* So now we'll just focus on the UK. The logic may well apply to many other nations. The numbers will be different.

On the 8th March 2020, the UK newspaper The Sunday Telegraph[48] ran an article in its electronic edition, headlined as *Leaving the EU is chance to cut £220bn in red tape.* The prospect of such savings is warming. This article has since disappeared from even electronic copies held on personal devices, but the number, whether it has a margin of error of even 100%, catches the eye and induces water into the eyes. Let us say that it is billions of pounds. How much of this is good regulation in terms of order and essential organisation we don't know? But what isn't in that category must be the bureaucracy devised by the Digital Icebergs that we continually talk about.

Figure 83
We're off

Regulation

The now-invisible article referenced above pointed the reader further to the UK Institute of Economic Affairs[49]. The IEA's website is full of pertinent information and quotes on and around the subject under discussion in this book. The website is well worth a visit. The IEA see *the enemy* as regulation and red tape. We see it as bureaucracy and red tape. These views are not far

---

[48] https://www.telegraph.co.uk/
[49] https://iea.org.uk/

apart. The outcomes of regulation and bureaucracy are the same, over-orderly and slow growth.

In the parlance of this book, we say:

Efficiency = Essential Organisation + Non-Essential Bureaucracy

In equivalent parlance, we can say:

Efficiency = Essential Regulation + Red Tape

When the last part of either equation above becomes negative (by definition), Efficiency declines.

Taxation costs

There is a specific monograph about the cost of tax collection and cost overheads to business in the UK on the IEA's website. The article is (Francis Chittenden 2010)[50]. Though dated 2010 the key messages are relevant.

- It's difficult to determine the cost of Tax Collection in the UK, but it is likely to be in the range of £15 - £20billion.
  - o We, in this book, can conclude that it's oversized, so a small percentage of savings will be big
- The cost of Tax Collection falls 16 times more heavily on the smallest businesses than the largest.
  - o In this book, we can comment that big is beautiful, noting that the first four letters of the word beautiful are the same as those of the word bureaucratic.
- There are, or were, then 463 pages of the overarching Finance Act.
  - o This book will undoubtedly conclude that those pages were produced by an IT system rather than chipped from stone.

 Tax at any level, whether on business or individuals, is an example of a necessary but overly complicated set of regulations and processes. So

Figure 84 Sharing

great is the complexity that there is a whole section of business known as Tax Experts and Tax Consultants with governing bodies to themselves regulate standards and professionalism. The complexity of the subject brings in the complexity of the solution. How much tax has to be paid and how much need not be paid is itself Big Business.

---

[50] Go to the IEA website: https://iea.org.uk/ and search on Tax Red Tape

Red tape again

Bureaucratic red tape is the destroyer of efficiency and the brake on growth, as we have said continuously. If you look inside an organisation, say a private company, you will see formal processes that define how the company produces its products and executes services to its customers. The standard procedures vary from industry to industry type. Sitting outside and on top of these are the rules and regulations, often laws, that the government has imposed. These come under various labels like:

- Fairtrade
  - This is interesting, especially within a trading block like the EU. Or Europe in general with the USA. Trade, fair or not, with China is often introduced into this discussion.
- An orderly market
  - Financial markets need to be executed within a defined order, especially the sequence of order. If a sell-buy instruction is not executed as a sell followed by a buy, funds may not be available for the buy.
- Legality
  - Is everything being executed within the rules of the law? Is data being correctly protected? Is insider trading happening?
- Tax levies
  - Taxes on businesses and individuals are inevitable, but if the 'giving' side is not minimal, the business's efficiency or individual is reduced. If the 'receiving' side's efficiency is not right, then the cost of collecting the taxes is too high.
- Social equality
  - Are women and men treated equally? Are ethnic minorities being treated fairly? Is age discrimination being practised?

All, of whatever kind, bring control. Whether that control is essential is our debate.

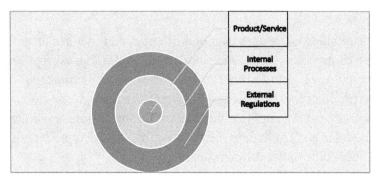

Figure 85 The bullseye of business

What is the essential cost, and what is the Red Tape Bureaucratic cost for a nation, a business, or an individual has been the subject of many studies? The main message is that IT is making it easier for the Red Tape Bureaucratic costs to grow. As fast as a given business improves its essential processes through IT, the counters come in from the government or the Digital Icebergs within that business's organisation. The cost incurred nationally is billions of pounds sterling.

Conclusions of this chapter

The real costs in absolute numbers of pounds sterling or US dollars of non-essential bureaucracy are often referenced in daily business and individual life but are not known with anything like even rough precision. It's a known unknown.

What we learn through feel and sense is that it is significant. It's probably on the increase as more-and-more redder-and-redder tape appears under the guise of regulation. The increasing use of IT facilitates this. IT is an enabler, just like steam was for older industries. But IT is also a disabler of productivity, profitability and progress. We gain but at a cost.

17.   Covid-19 and Bureaucracy

Abstract

We have already mentioned the Covid-19 pandemic, and this chapter highlights some examples of both good and bad bureaucracy that have occurred during the Covid-19 pandemic of 2020 and into 2021. No one had planned for the pandemic. No one had a plan to deal with the pandemic, so there was an opportunity for the *good, the bad, and the let's do something* to swing into action.

The scene

It is usually accepted that the Covid-19 pandemic originated in Wuhan, China, in 2019[51] and soon became a global nightmare in 2020 for the governments,

Figure 86 All the world is not a stage but a pandemic

democratic or otherwise, for our planet's nations. All nations were unprepared, but some were more prepared than others. Some had identified general risks from the likes of a flu pandemic or a sort-of new SARS outbreak, But none had real plans and the necessary processes to deal with an unseen and unforeseeable enemy like Covid-19. The scene was set for something big to happen, something that would shake the very foundations of civilisation. The curtain rose. Alas, the actors were not rehearsed, ready to enter the scene. The word pandemic was all over the media and was on everyone's lips. Somehow the word *plague* being seen as *passé*.

Many of the West's nations saw the initial threat as remote. Remote where the action was and remotely like a similar and significant event brewing in their domains. Risk Registers designated the happening as *unlikely,* which in plain-speak is *ignore it.* Anyway, if it does come knocking at our door or our neighbour's door, there will be time to deal with it. Such a position was, of course, a gross error of judgement both in terms of human lives, social activities and economic stability. But that is how we often deal with risks.

A cauldron of activities, many of them at panic levels, soon developed. These activities were at the frontline medical, and many needed skilled medical personnel to conduct them, especially badly infected treatment. But to support these skills, a massive system of supplying whatever was required had to be constructed. Supply chains for small items like clinical masks to hefty entities like

Figure 87 Pot au feu

---

[51] The actual first-occurance yet to be proven *beyond doubt* but assumed by many to be an animal market.

temporary hospitals had to be operational. For once, finance was not an option. It was a given; the bean counters were ignored, and *at all costs* was the order of the day.

In such a maelstrom of confusion and necessity, bureaucrats can positively or negatively work as we have so often debated in this book. It's a contest of Progress versus Delay. Which side has or will win the match-up is open to debate. Only the analysis that inevitably follows such a big event as the Covid-19 pandemic will finally decide. Then, no doubt, there will be a debate about that analysis. Mistakes were commonly made, critical decisions were often delayed, but progress in dealing with the pandemic's effects did happen. No nation was perfect in the way Covid-19 was tackled.

Good Covid-19 bureaucracy

It must be said with a booming voice that there are some heart-warming achievements.

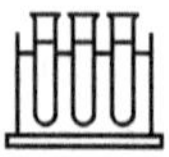

First, we must state there was a brilliant effort by scientists, microbiologists

Figure 88
Eureka

and those who understand viruses to design the vaccines as they did in 2020 to combat the pandemic in 2021. There could not have been a significant pushback by the Digital Icebergs. Scientists, as a general rule, want to practice their science. Their objective was clear. Their focus must have been total. No obstructions, either **Obstructive Bureaucracy** or excess **Cluterridge,** seem to have hindered their paths at any stage of their essential work. The end-results lead us to be sure of that.

Then after the scientists came the manufacture of the vaccines on a truly industrial scale. There seemed to be no gap between the vaccine's formulation, its testing, its safety checkouts and its bulk production. This organisational challenge must have been a colossal one, but somehow the good forces of bureaucracy combined to get the job done in the quickest time imaginable. However, the UK was faster than the EU (the big cheese itself) and its member states (27) in getting to this stage. Perhaps a reminder that often, when we have more decision-makers in the decision process, the time to decision gets extended. The same vaccines, same human beings, just more bureaucracy getting in the way, often under the umbrella of safety.

Finally, the vaccines had to be distributed and delivered to where the syringes

Figure 89
Maximum
torque not talk

were ready to give their doses into the needy's arms. The UK executed this task with excellent efficiency.

Help from the military with their combat-ready logistics was at hand again, proving that military discipline is the enemy of **Obstructive Bureaucracy** in times of crisis and trouble. We think of the military as having heavy bureaucracy in organisation and rule books and codes. This judgement is probably correct when not in action, but the military's ability to cut through is undoubted when in action.

An already (pre-Covid) stretched UK National Health Service (NHS) stepped-up to patient occupancy and care levels. Levels never experienced before, as did the health systems in many nations, whether national, regional or local. Bureaucracy was often thrown to the winds but not always. In enormous organisations and institutions, bureaucracy is part of the furniture and culture. Even in an extreme crisis, it can not step aside and not-exist.

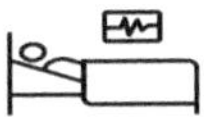

Figure 90 TLC

Bad Covid-19 bureaucracy

In the light of most of this book's focus on bad bureaucracy, or as we have called it, **Obstructive Bureaucracy.** Such a focus is exciting and entertaining. Here are some examples of how it raised its ugly head and other parts of its anatomy during the pandemic.

Educational bureaucracy

During 2020 and 2021, the Covid-19 pandemic caused children's education in the UK to be twice interrupted. Schools were partially closed, and scholars asked to remain at home unless their parents wanted them to attend. What follows below is a letter sent from a school to a parent. The text in *italics* has been added.

Dear *School*

Re: Health & Safety

I am writing to you following the increase in transmission and infection rates currently recorded across England.

You are, I am sure, aware that you have legal duties to protect the health, safety and welfare of your staff and pupils. Those duties arise under the following legislation: -

Sections 2 and 3 of the Health & Safety Act 1974

There are 4 Parts, 86 Paragraphs and 11 Scedules of this.

Regulations 3 and 8 of the Management of Health & Safety at Work Regulations 1999

There are 30 Paragraphs and 2 Schedules of this whole act.

Regulation 4 of the Personal Protective Equipment at Work Regulations 1992

There are 255 words in this.

Regulation 4 of the Workplace (Health, Safety & Welfare) Regulations 1992

There are 269 words in this.

Regulation 7 of the Control of Substances Hazardous to Health Regulations 2002

There are 974 words in this.

The most recent advice from SAGE is that schools should not open in January[52] other than for children of key workers and vulnerable children. This is because the scientific advice is that it is not safe for schools to open. There are new variants of Covid-19 that are highly infectious and infection rates have increased significantly since schools closed.

I appreciate that measures have been in place since September to allow the school to open, but according to SAGE, those measures may no longer be sufficient. They state in their most recent report: -

The introduction of Tier 4 measures in England combined with the school holidays will be informative of the strength of measures required to control the new variant but analysis of this will not be possible until mid-January.

Based on the above I do not believe that it is safe for me to return to teaching or supporting full classes at [name of school].

If I do attend [name of school] I believe that this will present a **serious** and **imminent** danger to my health and safety.

I am therefore writing to inform you that I am exercising my contractual right not to attend an unsafe place of work. I believe that not attending work in the

---

[52]
https://assets.publishing.service.gov.uk/government/uploads/system/uploads/attachment_data/file/948606/s0991-sage-meeting-74-covid-19.pdf

current circumstances is an appropriate step for me to take for the following reasons:

The **dangers** that are preventing me from attending work are the risk of contracting coronavirus and or spreading coronavirus to others.

The **person(s)** I am seeking to protect are myself, my family, our pupils, their families, my colleagues, their families and members of the public.

I believe that this danger is **serious** because coronavirus infection is potentially fatal and has already resulted in more than 73,512 deaths in the UK with a significant up surge in recent weeks.

I believe that, if I were to attend work, the danger would be **imminent** because before Christmas the highest infection rates were in children of school age, and the new variant may be more transmissible amongst students than previously.

I will be happy to return to the workplace once SAGE is satisfied that the R rate has decreased, scientific advice has been produced on safety measures required to make schools more "Covid secure", risk assessments have been updated and any necessary further safety measures implemented.

In the meantime, I am of course willing to carry out any of my duties that can be undertaken from my home, including planning, preparing and delivering on-line learning including supporting colleagues; and being in school supporting the learning of key worker and vulnerable children where necessary.

Yours sincerely, *Parents*

To just read the above letter is a significant task. It is a prime example of Information Overload. To research the background references is a daunting major task. The red references indicate the size of the iceberg below the waterline. To sign the letter, which implies that very few can do with confidence as a parent, you understand it is something that very few can do. What we have with this letter is a combination of pure bureaucracy and legal-speak and dictate. When brought together, they are a powerful negative bureaucratic force.

The letter is full to the brim with **Clutteridge.** When aimed at an ordinary citizen or family, the whole is overwhelming unless outside help is forthcoming.

Forms and more forms

Vaccinating everyone in the UK as quickly as possible is a challenge without precedent. One potential bottleneck was the actual application of the vaccine into the arms of the people. The task requires medically-trained personnel to be appropriately executed. There was a need to increase the number of 'jabbers' from a pool of former medical practitioners with inoculating patients' career-long experiences, not just in arms.

Figure 91 This won't hurt

Retired medical staff, especially doctors, tried to help because of their apparent skills. But many encountered a 'wall of bureaucracy' when volunteering to help as vaccinators.

It seems that re-vitalised medics were required to complete training courses in preventing radicalisation, fire safety and conflict resolution. None of the associated skills being necessary for the identified task or the identified urgency.

Some spoke of 15 different forms having to be filled in with lots of boxes ready for ticking. You can imagine the frustration of those willing to give of their time to a vital cause and hitting the wall, seeing the **Clutteridge.** You can further imagine the degree of the different ways of input for each 'form'. The options are:

- Fill in a set of fully online forms that can be submitted from a digital device.
- Forms that can be printed, filled in, and then sent somehow, perhaps attached to an email to somewhere.
- Online forms to apply for a paper form to be sent to the recipient. The legendary form-for-a-form.

The reception centre's effort to deal with the forms and process them is added to the input effort. Thereby 'the hidden wall', which is a sandpit for bureaucratic activities.

For bureaucracy, read change

When the UK was enduring the Covid-19 pandemic, like most other nations, the citizens were subjected to a lockdown of varying degrees. The lockdowns were the only way to control the virus's spread and the resulting illness before any significant effects of vaccinations. Lockdowns bought time, and time was needed.

So rules, laws, and guidelines were issued that defined what citizens could not do. By inference, what they could sometimes do within a particular region or locality. In less than one year into the pandemic since March 2020, the analysis showed that there had been 65 changes to the laws. The number of changes to the less-formal guidelines was almost certainly higher.

Figure 92 You will

Here we have an example of where bureaucracy does not delay and hinder progress but confuses the hell out of those at the receiving end of important information. Changes confuse when the rate at which they happen is faster than can be absorbed. People ask; *where are we now?* And *what's happening here?*

The good, the bad and *bugly*

Bugly is another new word. It's meant to imply the ugliness that results from bad bureaucracy.

It's the second week of January 2021, and the Covid-19 pandemic is rising and raging again almost everywhere. But the cavalry can be biologically heard riding over the vaccination hill. Vaccines are being manufactured and distributed to many nations. At first glance, you would think that size matters and the big countries would be leading the way. Here is what transpired and was reported.

Israel (a nation of 9.25 million) had inoculated more of its citizens than the total of Germany, France, and Italy put together (212 million combined). What could be a reason for the difference? Could it be that Israel is not part of an overarching governance structure (aka bad bureaucracy)? Israel has what is considered the best patient digital records system anywhere (aka good bureaucracy) or a combination of both (now known as a *bugly* effect).

Conclusion of this chapter.

As with any major event, there is a mixture of good and bad activities when people and organisations spring into action to deal with it.

Figure 93 The good usually win

Fortunately, and only time will tell, it appears that with the Covid-19 pandemic in the UK and it seems the same elsewhere, the good overcame the bad. The human desire to defeat bureaucracy often overcomes even the embedded bureaucracy that already exists. This factor hopefully happens when wars break out, major accidents happen, and pandemics occur. The signs are not all bad; they are encouraging.

The watchwords for an emergency is: Let's get the job done.

18.   Part 2 The Chipping-Away

Solutions to Obstructive Bureaucracy

19.   Where are we?

Abstract

We now take a checkpoint. We pull together key messages from the challenges that have been discussed in the first part of this book. It's a sort of bureaucratic attempt to organise the thinking, hopefully without excessive bureaucracy. The challenge is not simple.

You often get lost using the GPS in our cars because you haven't set it up properly.

So, we will attempt to set up the challenge correctly and proceed on the solution journey. Be prepared because this second part of the book is shorter than the first part because there isn't time to map out the possible solutions to the earlier part's challenge. This second part is a starting point that hopefully will prove useful to others.

Questioner: *Can I ask you a quick question?* **Answerer:** *You just have.*

Most questions are quick; it's the answers that take time, especially answers involving complex solutions.

Words are important

Words are indeed important and what they mean is even more critical.

We've already quoted the broken words of the ovoid-shaped Humpty Dumpty, but we list some of the words and phrases that we have used so far and try to group them to see a set of possible solutions that can be further explored. It's an attempt to identify the parts of the solution.

Words that describe, define and help us understand the challenge

In this context, The Challenge is meant to have a meaning of any of the list under the first heading below, sometimes several and often all.

Descriptive labels of the challenge

- Bureaucracy
- **Obstructive Bureaucracy**
- Regulation

Ways and means by which the challenge is practised

- Excessive input data
- Excessive output data

- Extra processes
- Stone, paper, digital IT
- **Clutteridge**
- Communications
- Complexity

Where the challenge is practised
- Nationally by governments
- Regionally and locally by authorities
- Locally by authorities
- Businesses
- By groups of like-minded individuals
- By individuals

Sideshows and fashions that promote the challenge
- Smart
- Artificial Intelligence (AI)

Effects of the challenge
- Reduced wealth and growth
- Organisation and structure, Good and Bad
- Increased costs

Instruments of the challenge
- Extra IT processes
- Excessive emails
- Social media

Players associated with the challenge
- Progressives
- Neutrals
- Luddites
- Digital icebergs
- Elite IT users
- Coping IT users

Restating our objective

At the beginning of this book, we were very clear that an advanced country like the UK has what we called a meagre economic growth rate. The UK has many positive factors that leave one feeling that the economic growth rates and the nation's wealth should be better. The citizens of the UK are not alone thinking like this.

 Repeatedly in Part 1 of this book, we stated that a factor, maybe the prime factor, holding back economic progress is **Obstructive Bureaucracy**. It gets in the way of efficiency and benefits, especially the benefits that IT can bring. IT is increasingly used to smother benefits.

This book aims to identify and root out the causes of IT's negative uses and begin the challenge to describe how these root causes can be reduced and, if possible, eradicated.

Beginning to understand the root causes of Obstructive Bureaucracy

In Part 1 of this book, we rambled on about the underlying causes and from the list above, it is evident that there are many of these causes around. We are faced with a complex and diverse overall challenge. So be it.

So we're going to work through the list section by section and see what can be done.

Descriptive labels of the challenge

- Bureaucracy
- **Obstructive Bureaucracy**
- Regulation

Part 1 of this book introduces and covers these practices and how they have been around since the Stone Age. We have introduced and defined the *newish* term **Obstructive Bureaucracy** in Chapter: 10, The dark art of bureaucracy. We don't need a chapter on this part of the challenge. We do on the next set, though.

Summary of this chapter

The challenge of **Obstructive Bureaucracy** is complex. There are many underlying causes. Therefore the overall solution is a wide one. As we have listed, there are many parts to the challenge of reducing bureaucracy. There is a constant increase in these many parts because of human ingenuity and innovation. The beast is being fed, and so the solution is multi-headed like the multi-headed Hydra of Greek mythology.

20.   Ways and means by which the challenge is practised

Abstract

We're now going to look very briefly at how our IT systems today are specified and designed. The look will be an overview of what is a complicated activity. Over-specified can sometimes be a better description of what can happen. We have discussed the extras that cost in real wealth terms and in time, as discussed in previous chapters.

The set of practices

These are were listed above:

- Excessive input data
- Excessive output data
- Extra processes
- Stone, paper, digital IT
- Communications
- Complexity

Before diving in and tackling each one, we should step back and discuss how an IT system with its processes is defined and designed today, how it is engineered. This will seem a ramble as we begin and proceed, but we are looking for root causes, and some of these are deep.

The Business-IT Gap

The Business-IT Gap has been around for many years. In essence, you have two parties:

1. Businesspersons who drive a business and the likes of a government. They know the processes of a company and the products and services. They do not understand the full workings of IT. To them, some are mysteries.
2. IT professionals who know IT's workings but do not understand the full workings of a company's processes or the products and services.

Figure 94 I thought you meant this? No I meant that!

Listing some characteristics for consideration:

- Businesspersons speak in business-speak.
- IT persons speak in IT-speak.
- Both languages are heavily endowed with jargon.
- Some businesses move slowly.
- IT never moves gradually.

Some of the mismatches, as above, end up resulting in a further mismatch between what the company wants and what IT provides. It usually takes time for the mismatch to be spotted. The larger the project to deliver a system, the greater the chances of a mismatch occurring. National projects are particularly susceptible.

Into the Business-IT Gap rides the cavalry, the riders of which are known as Business Analysts. These professionals explore with the businesspersons what they want and define what they think they want in languages, frameworks and

diagrams of their own using specific tooling. The IT professionals then have to take these definitions and decompose them into strings of zeros and ones (digitise, you might say) representing the programs (apps) and the system's data. Like in any step process, and there are quite a few depending on the IT development process being used, errors occur at the steps' interfaces. This is typical IT.

Figure 95 IT has a lot of horsepower

But, there is a specific window in the process at which the extras can creep in. It's what we might call a Bureaucracy Window.

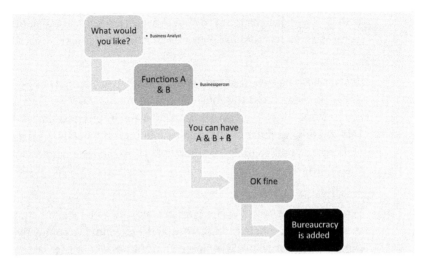

From such simple and often innocent conversations, extra functions are inserted, usually under the radar of common sense and what it means when implemented.

Excessive input data

Extra functions, extra input data will be asked for from the end-user, thereby slowing down the end-user and the overall process in terms of time-to-execute.

More is less.

Excessive output data

The extra data from above has to be stored and represented as information. Or, it may be presented elsewhere to many others even though they have not asked for it.

More is more than less.

Extra processes

These can be a real brake on the productivity of the user. He or she has to handle another set of steps. In the olden days, putting in an extra process meant adding additional forms, so it was significant to induce an extra bureaucratic effort into a function. Also, an extra step in the manufacturing process was a pretty obvious addition. It was and still is an additional physical task, whether manual or automated. But now,

Figure 96
Not a lot
more

with IT, when designing, say, online services, it is easy. Extra inputs and outputs asked for from the end-user. **Clutteridge** appears.

Stone, paper, Digital IT

There's nothing new in putting in extra steps, data, outputs as was asked for above. In olden times this must have gone on. But, now we have IT with its ease-of-use, it's ever-growing capabilities and its business analysts. As we have said, these have made IT a fantastic sandpit for the bureaucrats and Digital Icebergs to practice their **Obstructive Bureaucracy** and fill the sandpit with their **Clutteridge.**

Communications

We now live in a world where we can make the general statement that; everything is connected to everyone and *everyone.* The connectivity is 100%. Connectivity not only at the physical cable level where each cable fits into a global network. But connectivity at a logical level where each node in that worldwide network has an address and many, many applications can exchange data, events, and transactions. Therefore, it is easy for anyone designing an IT system to use more of this connectivity than is necessary. The extra steps and inputs, and outputs that we have referenced above can be added.

Figure 97 Are we really all in this together?

Complexity

We have covered some of this topic before, but it's worth noting that there are states that an IT system can be in as regards its complexity.

- It can be *by design* just as simple and complex as is needed for it to do its essential job.
- It can be too complex by design to do its essential job and is, therefore, exhibits **Obstructive Bureaucracy**.

- It was designed to be as simple as possible and has become overly-complex because of what we can call **Creeping Complexity**. New functionality has been added (often under the umbrella of improvement, becoming Smart, or *as asked for by our users)*. IT systems become inundated by upgrades, new versions, fixes (of bugs). They are rarely static, and in the onward rush, you can decide whether it's an upward or downward rush; they change. It is this change that brings about complexity and often adds to the bureaucracy. Those end-users who can just cope with the complexities of the system may now not be able to.

> Questioner: Do you have the answer to the question that I have asked?
>
> Answerer: Could you repeat the question, please?
>
> Questioner after repeating: Do you now have the answer?
>
> Answerer: Could you repeat the question again, please?
>
> Questioner after repeating yet again: Do you have the answer to the question yet?
>
> Answerer: I don't have an answer because I don't understand the question. It's too complex.

Summary of this chapter

Try to understand what the basic requirements are so that anything functionally above these is excessive and extra. It is **Clutteridge.** It is so easy to add these extras to an IT system because the capability of IT is vast, often cheap, and these extras are:

Key questions

1. Are these extras *nice-to-haves* and *examples of the considerable range of bells and whistles that IT offers?*
2. What effect do these extra inputs, outputs and processes have on the efficiency of the end-users? What extra time do they need the end-user to spend?
3. Is this whole system too complicated for the minimal, where minimal implies the lowest capable, end-user to understand the number of options for input and outputs available to them?

A few questions asked at the right time can help produce better answers and better systems.

21.   Where the challenge is practised

Abstract

We will explore the sources of **Obstructive Bureaucracy**, the epicentres, the places within an organisation from where it spreads its tentacles and engulf its users. We'll take a top-down view starting with the national government then the production hubs and factories (aka offices) where **Clutteridge** is mined and produced.

Nationally by governments

In the first part of this book, we discussed that the reach of government

Figure 98
Please fill
me in

systems, sometimes based upon regulation, is into the whole population. Directly into citizens and indirectly into infants until they grow into end-users. So if any government system is overly-bureaucratic, the nation's efficiency is bound to be affected adversely. Many government systems are migrating from a paper base to an IT digital base. Paper forms are becoming screen forms. As this transformation happens, it is very tempting to enhance the inputs and outputs and ask for more data and display more information. The old forms sometimes disappear.

So as end-users use these systems and grapple with the newness experience, they must efficiently use their time on only necessary actions. Anything else is a waste of their time. One second wasted per user per year has a massive multiplier associated with it.

Some national systems' complexity is daunting for some end-users who are not digitally adept. Those who are not digitally adept are a much higher proportion of a modern nation than imagined. The root cause of this is often due to the complexity of the regulation. We have discussed that tax in many countries is a complex labyrinth of pathways with many potholes. Once an end-user answers an online question that shunts them from the main path, the time spent figuring out what extra data is needed can be considerable. Frustration results, errors are made, and end-goals are not reached.

Regionally and locally by authorities

Most countries are divided into states, counties, departments, provinces.

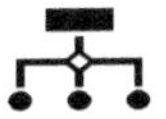

Figure 99 It's
the system

Empires, of course, had colonies and provinces; they were no doubt hotbeds of bureaucracy. Within the boundaries of the sub-national authorities exist some local authorities. Wherever the national government's big-foot does not tread, the lower power in question has an organisation. Where the smaller-foot of the higher authority does not gently walk, the lower power has an organisation. The system is hierarchical, but there is the potential for bureaucratic practices to sprout and take hold at each level. IT is available to all levels, even the lower local levels, since base functions like email are ubiquitous and often without direct costs.

Figure 100 I want to change.

Some nations have tax systems and regulation below the national level, thereby putting processes in place to collect the tax based upon sales or property types and sizes. Once again, there are big multipliers for the effects of bureaucracy. At these levels also exist such functions and process for planning, especially local developments of businesses and home dwellings. These are seen by many as prime bases for our Digital Icebergs to practise **Obstructive Bureaucracy**. The landscape is one of:

- the forms to be filled correctly,
- reviews and meetings to take place,
- decisions to be made or delayed,
- appeals to be heard,
- further data to be submitted,
- escalations to be launched,
- and the legal representatives to be commissioned.

The steps in the process seem to be endless. The opportunity for IT systems to be employed to enable efficiency is enticing.

Businesses

When we think of economic growth, we think of the businesses that make up a country's commercial substance. These are the real creators of wealth, and they are the source of products and services. At one end of the business scale, they are mega, employ thousands of people and have annual turnovers in the millions and millions. Once again, the multipliers are significant because of their size. At the other end, a business can be a corner shop or an individual in a home office. The multipliers are substantial because of the numbers involved.

Big business

Large businesses have to have organisation and structure. How much is a matter of more debate and literature than the Universe can hold? It's also a matter of how focused a given business is and how many different offerings it has. Also, where its physical presence is. Suppose you consider the UK's National Health Service to be a business. In that case, it executes the same processes all across the UK. If you think of a motor manufacturing business, it probably has one assembly plant somewhere within a country. If a company is global, then there may be instances of that business in many countries.

Figure 101 Growth begats growth

From the above jumble of considerations comes the oft-asked question: *How much centralisation and control should exist?* Some businesses have cyclic answers. Every five years say the pendulum has swung too far towards centralisation, and there is a swing back towards devolution and local empowerment. Some businesses are always centralised, some always decentralised. In this book, we're not going to discuss the merits of these options, and we are interested in bureaucracy and how it thrives on the backs of IT and IT's capabilities.

IT is everywhere in any business, as we have said. Suppose you are in a Head Quarters function. Do you control the company's IT rigidity from the centre or allow it to be devolved to the divisions and foreign locations? It is not just the IT infrastructure like servers and networks that can be controlled but the systems and applications. These latter softer items allow bureaucracy to build up because they are hard to control when someone in a foreign land or a particular division at home begins to get hooked-on extras. Opposed to this, if the centre's control is tight, the end-users see rigid processes with excessive disciplines that they see as our old enemy **Obstructive Bureaucracy**. The tight control becomes the bureaucratic focus. All sorts of elements of **Clutteridge** appear in the name of the management. Standards manuals are issued with choice instructions that begin with *You will*.

Figure 102 I'm here to Help

As IT infrastructure has changed with the emergence of the cheap chip and the Cloud, it has meant that IT has left the Data Centre with its big mainframes and fixed networks. It has been distributed everywhere and seemingly to everyone, as we have discussed. IT is now so difficult to control and as apps appear everywhere, so does bureaucracy, as we have again discussed.

Small business

At the other end of our business size scale, the corner shop and the home office business has been the recipients of what we can call; *IT for Everyone*. An apparent boom this has been for the affordability of a business's website, allowing that business to have application functions beyond its dreams some years ago. Many of these functions, say like online ordering or printing a pamphlet, are provided by software packages with a wide range of processes. It's very attractive for small businesses to enable these. They can add-up to bureaucracy for the small business and its customers.

Figure 103 Shop here

Small businesses are often started by entrepreneurs who don't recognise bureaucracy and anything that stands in the way of them successfully building their business. But at some point, there need to be formal processes, and it's a golden opportunity for the Digital Icebergs to appear. The spirit of *just do it* is tempered with what seems like an overly-constraining process. Success brings its negatives.

Merging businesses

It's interesting to consider what happens when a big business acquires a small business and absorbs it into its organisation. The systems of the big business will probably replace the systems of the small business. Those who have to endure the change will see the new methods as overly-bureaucratic. The small business's employees and possibly customers will feel the effects of heavier processes and see them as having impeded the business's agility. The agility that made it grow and perhaps why the larger company paid good money for the smaller one.

Figure 104 I'm less agile than I was

Individuals

These are individuals who are executing something for their purposes, not the purposes of the business that employs them. They are the ones who seem to be able to send an email every other minute with baseless information in it to a contact list that appears to exceed the population of the Universe. They are the ones who can post something on a social media site, including a set of photographs on the hour every hour. They generate **Clutteridge** at a fantastic pace and with remarkable regularity.

Individuals post their interest on a topic on a website, either directly ticking a box indicating that they are interested in the price of a product or service.

Sometimes they just search for something on a website and leave their email address or become a registered member. They then have opened to door to continued contact and further information. They then, as we have said earlier, have to endure the contact or unsubscribe their interested. Both of which consume time and are sometimes impossible. Time that is personal and not productive. In the end, this is **Obstructive Bureaucracy** in action because the individual is obstructed from spending his or her free time as he or she decides. This is an IT system, of some sort, making them spend their time with its excesses.

Figure 105
My cup and
inbox run
over

Messages from this chapter

The challenge of bureaucracy and, in particular, **Obstructive Bureaucracy** is a vast playing field on which governments, businesses big and small, and individuals can practice.

Key messages are:

1. If you are a government and want your citizens to be productive, do not impose upon them IT systems that exhibit **Obstructive Bureaucracy**. Don't cause them to spend time with unessential input, output and processes. The time of individuals is precious to that individual. When added together, it is enormously productive.
2. If you are a business and want your employees to be productive, do not ask them to operate IT systems that impact your business's efficiency. An extra input or screen has a significant knock-on effect.
3. Suppose you are an individual demonstrating prolific output to others. In that case, it is great fun but wastes a lot of the time of others, many of whom you may not know.

22.   Sideshows and fashions that promote the challenge

Abstract

This chapter investigates how the labels *Smart* and *Artificial Intelligence* are parts of the current IT scene and can lead to obstructive practices and **Obstructive Bureaucracy** under cover of fashionable names.

Recapping

As this book was written, it was tempting to tell the reader that Smart and Artificial Intelligence AI subjects have been covered concerning **Obstructive Bureaucracy** in two previous chapters. Chapter 15 Bureaucracy makes my eyes smart, and Chapter 8 How information

Figure 106 Diving deeper

is manufactured, stored and distributed. That is so, but it's worth diving a little deeper into both of these subjects to understand how they are the Trojan Horses of today regarding stealth and deceit.

Smart and AI are sometimes linked by the use of AI in a system to make it even smarter.

Smart

As we have discussed, Smart means when you boil down to that fact that you have or intend to throw a bunch of chips, programming and storage at something. To make it more complicated, but hopefully better. The meaning of *better* is debatable. The intention is to make it a system with more functionality and more apparent capabilities. The subject in question being endowed with the smart property might be as huge as a city with a transport system down to something as small as a mobile phone.

The goal is to join up various components and pieces, big or small, so that the whole is smarter and is hopefully more dynamic. The new system optimises resources to give better throughput. Such an aim seems to be an anti-bureaucratic goal and should be applauded. For instance, all drivers have to

Figure 107 Chips under the bridge

register to enter a city or cross a toll bridge; this is a task. If you cannot go through a toll booth unless you have registered previously, you are experiencing **Obstructive Bureaucracy**.

Figure 108 All-in-One

Suppose you have a smartphone with a camera, phone, email, and Internet capability. In that case, you have to have an email address to upload photographs to the cloud, and you don't want to experience **Obstructive Bureaucracy**. Why do you need all of these functions? You have to learn, and often relearn, how you use each function. There is challenging, and it is more complicated than it should be.

The city, the bridge, or the phone may be smarter and more efficient and convenient, but the processes' inputs and outputs are more significant for the end-user. Time has to be spent by the user in getting to be part of the smart new world. Sometimes, unless you spend time, the system obstructs you from asking for more and more information about who you are and what you are doing. The system may be smart, but do you want it to be?

The art of not being Smart

Technology is moving very fast, but the arts/humanities seem so slow in comparison. Why is this? Apart from some of the visual arts, the arts seem to be immune to technology like many other commerce and society sectors.

- We get a myriad of new songs but so few operas and shows. We have discussed this previously.
- We get so many soundbites but so few real plays. Also, this has been discussed.
- There are many new dance styles (well, sort of) but so few new ballets.

Perhaps the arts are smarter than smart[53] and untrammelled by the bureaucracy that technology provides. The word untrammelled is not a new word and means without clutter. The arts do not allow **Clutteridge** to darken their doorstep. We need new words to help us understand **Obstructive Bureaucracy**, especially concerning artistic progress. We have coined **Clutteridge,** and we now unearth ***untrammelled,*** which means 'not deprived of freedom of action or expression; not restricted or hampered'. Untrammelled means 'not subject to the restrictions of **Clutteridge** and the forces of **Obstructive Bureaucracy**. Perhaps the arts know something that the sciences do not. The arts are more selective and surprisingly less seduced by fashions.

---

[53]It is noticeable that art is the last three letters of smart.

Artificial Intelligence (AI)

AI has been around for many years. For a while, it was called Machine

Intelligence. These days AI often is the label for anything that is not natural or direct human intelligence. In short, this means the use of IT to produce what appears to be intelligence. It can also imply robotics, but the brainpower is still based upon the chip's capabilities. Some fear that the chip's capabilities will either

Figure 109 Who's in charge?

accidentally or by design become dangerous and overpowering to our existence. Some fear that we shall be overtaken by brains more extensive than our natural brains. Time will tell what will happen. If you wait long enough, anything and everything will happen. So, it's a matter of time. No doubt, these super brains will practice bureaucracy, and this will slow them down. We can but hope. Since they have been programmed at the start by human programmers, they will almost certainly be tainted with bureaucratic routines.

What have computers done for us and still do for us?

We stated earlier that AI is a fashion. Well, so it is. But like many fashions, it has been around for years as a segment of Computer Science.

If you stand back and consider what characterises computers they are;

1. Fast and consistently getting more rapid, especially when working in parallel in many numbers on a single problem.
2. Programmable with rules of the desired precise and specific behaviour.
3. Good at retaining data because they have increasingly large memories which can be indexed.
4. Accurate because they don't make mistakes. Well, if you assume that perfect programming and infinitely thorough testing is standard. If you do, you have probably never written a computer program.
5. Reliable because they just keep working, apart from upgrades are being applied. You might want to consider looking into built-in obsolescence if you think computers have an infinite lifespan.

It is the combination of 2 and 3 above that is intriguing. It begins to attract the attention of those who are seeking to develop something new like AI. The rules by which computers work are set in stone, just like the chips of ancient times by programming protocols. The instructions or programs execute on elements of data in an exact fashion. They compare data elements, move data elements, store data elements and produce information based on the precise analysis. The intelligence and logic of the human mind, often many combined-minds, is transposed into chip jargon, and the chips do the rest, so to speak. Yes, nowadays, the chips can speak. There are logical sequences in the programming like:

- If this,
- then that,
- if there is not a 1 in that there,
- and the time is noon.

Although the above is quite simple, it seems very vague because we can't see the data being acted upon, and the sequence of the process itself is very rigid. You can use logic infinitely more complicated than that above to achieve all kinds of feats of execution and the retrieval of information. Imagine that we have some defined logic, and this is a set of rules that has been programmed. This logic can analyse data and extract information, say patterns, and have virtually new data. We now have a powerful potential for seeking answers to deep questions. Questions that we have pondered since time began.

The only knowns are knowns

We are now going to go into Rumsfeld-speak and say that we can:

- Determine known-knowns again or
- Determine known-unknowns for the first time or
- Surprise ourselves by finding unknown-unknowns

Figure 110
Anyone
there?

So the logic determined by human intelligence, skills and experience finds us some patterns in the data that we suspected were there but were not identified. It was too difficult to determine them even for the best minds of the age. Now the answers to some questions are identified. The computer, with its chips, programming and data, has done its job. If you run the logic against the same data again, it will do the same job and return the same information. So you will have to improve the reasoning logic if you want to find an unknown-unknown and trawl through shedloads of data. But, you don't know what you are seeking, by definition. It is beyond the human abilities and skills available.

But what if the computer system itself could learn from what it has done and itself upgrade the logic to at least begin a search for the unknown-unknown. Due to its tireless efforts, it could gradually grind away at the task and get closer to the goal. Perhaps through trial and error, but it has great speed, is accurate and is reliable. It has endurance and doesn't tire. All it needs is time and a few volts of electricity. The possibilities are infinite, but alas, we do not know what infinity is.

Figure 111 I have a mind of my own, I think?

Instead of programming a computer to analyse data to determine a pattern, you might program it to execute 100 tasks. You might leave a window in the logic for the robot to try a task of its own. Itself deciding based upon its experiences from the new data collected from all the millions of times the 100 tasks have been executed. You allow the robot to learn new tricks. There's a saying that *you can't teach an old dog new tricks.* In straightforward terms, the battle cry of AI is *you can teach a new computer unknown tricks.*

For every upside and downside

There are two potential downsides to all of this AI expansion of logic. Both are relevant to our fight against bureaucracy.

Artificial Obstructive Bureaucracy

In seeking out the unknown unknowns, the AI may create bureaucracy in the form of excessive information or extra tasks for end-users to execute. AI may put in additional steps in a process because it has learned that the original set of functions could be improved so that it doesn't realise it is bureaucratic as we have defined bureaucracy.

The AI may then ask the robot to execute something that no one had ever thought could be actionable. The results could be very damaging.

In the year 1968, a film called 2001 A Space Odyssey was released. Almost 20 years after the date in its title, the film seems way ahead of its time and is visionary. The spacecraft central to the plot is controlled by a massive brain (both in physical size and logic power) called HAL. HAL is there to help the astronauts in everything that they do. He, or she, is programmed to do this. But alas, HAL is not free from errors and decides to execute some logic of his or her own making. The results are not what the astronauts expect.

Figure 112 Hope springs eternal

The jury is out, and maybe this will be the case for some times, but we potentially have with AI is a new breed of our Digital Icebergs. There is an opportunity for the system to execute and become bureaucratic and operate in a bureaucratic way. Perhaps an AI system is the pure instantiation of a Digital Iceberg? The perfection of the imperfections that we call bureaucracy. Suppose these systems uncover unknown-unknowns and execute tasks that have never been imagined even by our race's most intelligent. In that case, their behaviour is an unknown-unknown all round. Do we have the perfect Catch 22 situation?

The prospect is indeed a known-unknown when you boil it down. And when you boil it down even further, Artificial Intelligence is computer programming that is meant to reveal what Human Intelligence and imagination cannot. Surprises may result[54]. If you don't think that they will result, argue with this logic, naturally or artificially.

Programming is an uncertain process; some might say and uncertain science or even uneasy art. The uncertainty comes from the outcomes that are not planned as a result of its execution. These are what we call 'bugs'. They are unintended consequences not designed in or out by the designer or errors made by the programmers who have not understood the design. They are not

Figure 113 I'm into everything

caught in the testing, proving and trialling the software and the system that runs it. They are the Achilles Heel of IT. No matter how much software is wished for, prayed for or even deluged with money, it is never 100% perfect. There is always that small delta, or even sometimes a big delta, that makes it imperfect.

Now, consider further what is happening with AI. Programmers are programming an AI system, be it a computer, a robot or a big network of logically connected intelligence. Their programming allows the AI system to reprogram itself and become a different system. The original software has unforeseen logic errors like paths that have not been anticipated and thereby not tested and proved. One of these rogue routines now starts to produce its routine, and the chances are that this will be a rogue routine whose activity and outcomes could be benign or dangerous. In our context, bureaucratic to the degree that adds bureaucracy on top of bureaucracy and who is being bureaucratic isn't her or she or them it is it.

We shall live in exciting times when AI becomes our bureaucratic enemy number one or even threatens us all in more dangerous ways. It's hard to say when such times will arrive. Perhaps they have come, and we don't even know.

---

[54] If we are really devlish we might remark that this definition of AI is also applicable to programming and the way that bugs appear.

Messages from this chapter

The messages concerning our fight with Obstructive are simple:

1. IT is often driven by fashions and jargon that is not fully understood by businesses and individuals. The potential for **Obstructive Bureaucracy** to creep into the main thrust of these fashions is real. It is significant and is often counter-productive.

2. The benefits of AI are potentially significant. AI allows a business to ask for something unknown. A business needs to be careful to get what it didn't ask for because it doesn't know what it doesn't know. The result may be **Obstructive Bureaucracy** in a new form. We shall see; the jury is out, so until they do decide, do not trust programming. And certainly do not trust those who say that you can trust it.

Figure 114 Time, if it still exists, will tell

23.   Effects of the challenge

Abstract

We now consider how bureaucracy and Obstructive Bureaucracy's challenge puts a drag factor on nations' wealth and citizens. We don't quantify this but point to areas where it might be happening.

Reduced wealth and growth

At the start of this book, we highlighted that the UK and many other advanced nations have what we call the stigma of a meagre economic growth rate. We have at our fingertips and eyes the full gambit of what we call IT. Businesses invest heavily in this technology, but still, somehow, the growth numbers are small if not zero. How much companies spend on IT varies from business to business. Some have an IT budget of a few percentages of turnover, some an IT budget of 10% plus.

IT is everywhere. No business is immune from its capabilities and its costs. Some companies only exist because of IT. The credit card business is a good example. Apart from the physical cards themselves, everything is virtual and transactional in an electronic sense. Some companies that are real-time customer-facing don't work if their IT systems don't work. If you are in an airport check-in queue or supermarket check-out queue and the system is down, there is probably no manual back-up system.

There are two components to the cost of IT.

1. The costs to keep the businesses running with the current processes. These we can call Operations Costs.
2. The cost to make the businesses run better, more efficiently, more responsively and with more profits. These we can call the development costs.

Obstructive Bureaucracy occurs in 1 above and inflates the Operational Costs and diminishes the operational benefits and profits. But it originates in 2 above. It has been directly designed into the processes because of the extras that we have discussed previously. It has been developed indirectly because the process operators, including the general public, have adopted inefficient practices and spend more time on a process than expected. This inefficiency, as we have said previously, is often creeping bureaucracy. At the business or IT level, the system's original design and its processes were not tight enough to prevent the creep. Whether national or through to a small business, the costs are higher and the benefits less. The economic and financial growth suppressed.

There is another way that a business's growth is suppressed, and bureaucracy plays a negative part. Most companies need to change to meet new regulations, react to competitive market pressures and the shortage or abundance of skills and labour. It is often the case that IT systems have to be upgraded or sometimes even replaced to meet such business challenges. The speed with which this can happen is key to the growth of the business. **Obstructive Bureaucracy** often appears when the focus is on change, significantly change to IT. We can liken the IT systems of a company to a Christmas tree with many baubles on it. A change represents a new bauble. A variety makes decisions on where the trinket will is placed on the tree of experts. But eventually, there are no spare places on the branches for the new babbles. Or, worse still, the positioning of one bauble causes the tree to fall over because it is unstable. **Clutteridge** has cluttered the tree.

Figure 115 Don't overload

Organisation and structure

Any business or government establishment, no matter what size, has to have some organisation or structure, individuals acting as individuals don't. Within the organisation is the function we have been calling IT.

For our discussions of bureaucracy, we can think of a two-part organisation; business and IT. The big question for many companies is; should the IT function be part of the business structure, or should it be stand-alone? We have previously posed the question of central or decentralised control and often bureaucracy, obstructive or not? IT is always part of the business, even for an IT enterprise. Should sit inside the business divisions say, or be s division on its own.

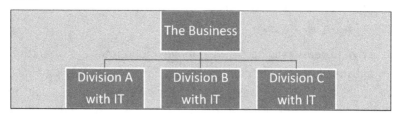

Figure 116 Divisional IT

Or

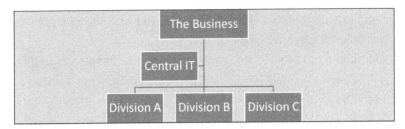

Figure 117 Central IT

The first model above allows for local autonomy and local control. The second model above allows for corporate independence and control. But which model is the best breeding ground for **Obstructive Bureaucracy?** We asked this question in a different format before. Still, the answer is probably the second because it dictates the systems. The standard functions like email, personnel, wages, and property services have to be more general or term *functionally more comprehensive* to serve all the divisions.

Increased costs

The provision of IT functions is a costly item for a business. Some business executives see them as overhead. The costs can be quite easily computed and made up of hardware, software licenses, network, maintenance, IT operations, training and development. IT supports the business processes, so the IT systems' efficiency is of significance in business efficiency. But when

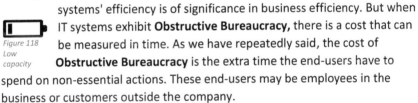

Figure 118 Low capacity

IT systems exhibit **Obstructive Bureaucracy,** there is a cost that can be measured in time. As we have repeatedly said, the cost of **Obstructive Bureaucracy** is the extra time the end-users have to spend on non-essential actions. These end-users may be employees in the business or customers outside the company.

The full costs are not easy to assemble. It's not difficult to measure the time-waste costs of employees within the business, but it is challenging even to assess the costs of lost time for customers. For a national governmental system, these can be many. No wonder a nation can experience low economic growth.

Messages from this chapter

There are enormous benefits for a business from the correct use of IT. The costs often appear to be high and are sometimes considered overheads.

1. Where IT fits in the organisational structure of a business is not always clear, especially when **Obstructive Bureaucracy** is allowed to flourish and influence the decision.
2. The hidden costs occurred when this happens and can be significant, not just extra costs but in lost opportunities. The ability of a business to make necessary changes and thereby grow can be impeded by **Obstructive Bureaucracy**. Beware! Digital Icebergs are everywhere.

24.   Chipping away at the iceberg

Abstract

We now have an understanding of the challenge of **Obstructive Bureaucracy,** where and how it manifests itself. It is time to begin to propose a set of antidotes to the adverse effects of bureaucracy in IT systems that are used by businesses and by individuals.

> **Identify your problems but give your power and energy to solutions** – Tony Robbins author (1960 and going as at 2020)

What have we got to do?

In earlier chapters, we have continuously described the perpetrators of bureaucracy and, in particular, the harmful practice of **Obstructive Bureaucracy** as performed by Digital Icebergs.

Obstructive Bureaucracy must be reduced within and around many digital IT systems based upon the microchip's power and capabilities. It matters for all types and sizes of a system, from national governmental systems down to the systems individuals use for social purposes. Unless systems are cleansed of

extras, excesses, and nice-to-haves and reduced to essential functionality, a nation or a business's growth will be impacted. This objective has become so crucial in the chip-driven world that we inhabit. Business systems are not entertainment. They are the lifeblood of an economy and are becoming more and more so.

Figure 119 This act needs cleaning up

What will happen if we don't do anything?

Unless we restrain and hopefully eliminate **Obstructive Bureaucracy,** it is not hard to imagine a time when everyone is inundated with millions of emails per day. Whether for business reasons or personal reasons, individuals spend all their awake hours merely dealing with these emails and not becoming wiser or wealthier. It is not hard to imagine a customer having to fill in 20 screens of input to buy a product on the Internet. The data captured being bigger and bigger in its size and scope, and the analysis of this data is more profound and more in-depth with thinner and thinner connection with real life.

We need to ensure that the ever-increasing functionality and availability of IT is used productively for business. It is not the sandpit of those who want to deliberately or indirectly over-engineer IT systems. Design them to become beautiful examples of buildings based upon the baroque architectural style that is very pleasant on the eye but not suited to modern office efficiencies.

The two-headed attack – Orthros

Orthros was a two-headed monster dog in Greek mythology. His place in Greek mythology is cemented because he was slain by Heracles, who was Hercules in the Roman world. It will indeed take a Herculean effort to eradicate the Obstructive Bureaucracy monster from our businesses and society. We suggest that this will tale a two-headed attack. The one head we'll call Essential Design (and redesign) the other we'll call Cultural Change. The two are inevitably interdependent.

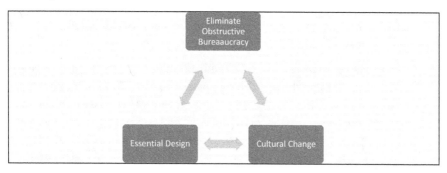

Figure 120 The Herculean two-headed attack

If we think of real icebergs, we can say that there are two ways that we can reduce their size and, therefore, their dangers.

1. Essential Design: we chip away at them to reduce their bulk, and the resulting chips float harmlessly away. Similarly, we minimise **Obstructive Bureaucracy** by eliminating it from systems bit-by-bit (sometimes literally) and thereby nullifying its effects.
2. Cultural Change: Icebergs disappear because they melt. So we have to warm up the sea around them. This task is significant and is a long term goal.

The next two chapters expand on each of the above and point a way forward.

Messages from this chapter

There are two main messages from this chapter.

1. We need to tackle the Obstructive Beaurocracy challenge across two fronts.

2. The task is an enormous one. But then the prize of increased economic growth and wealth is significant also.

If two wrongs don't make a right, then try three – Laurence J Peter writer
(1919 to 1990)

25. Essential Design – part of the answer

Abstract

This chapter identifies what can be done by system designers, both at the business and the technology levels, to reduce **Obstructive Bureaucracy.** How essentials are the design's focus rather than overly-heavy functionality with its burdens on the end-user and the business owners. This involves chipping away and making the non-essentials smaller, chip by chip. These are little efforts by those who design and implement IT systems. They will need strong adherence to the continuous and frequent question; *is this data or this end-user activity essential?*

'Enough is enough is enough is enough' – words from the song No More Tears by Paul Jabara and Bruce Roberts

Lean and mean

In the physical engineering world, say the making of automobiles or white household goods, there are terms called Lean Manufacturing or Lean Production. These ways of working methodically ensure that only essential and sufficient activities happen when something is manufactured or produced. You might use the slogan *Just Enough.*

Figure 121
The bare bone

The *just enough* is for the production of the end-product, not the end-product. The end-product could be over-specified and, therefore, over-engineered. We have repeatedly put forward the proposition that many of the interfaces they use are over-engineered from an end-user efficiency perspective. Often over-engineered by a margin that we have called bureaucracy, this is **Obstructive Bureaucracy**, which reduces efficiency in one form or another. Something is amiss and is missing in the design and implementation process of many IT systems.

The wrong experts for the job

The business wants a rich system solution at a low cost. The business analysts wish for a rich system solution and define one keeping some costs in mind. The IT system architects want a rich system solution and design one keeping fewer cost constraints in mind. This desire for richness and over-engineering continues until the deployment of the system. It is into this vat of expectation that the Digital Icebergs apply their deeds, and **Obstructive Bureaucracy** takes a foothold.

Figure 122
The old ways are the best

There is little focus on how efficient the end-users will be and how free from bureaucracy they will be using the system. Oh, yes, the business and technology designers will shout. But, just think of the systems you interface with and how much time you waste dealing with options, choices, extras and the like. What we have called **Clutteridge** is in most systems. How often do you receive a digital something that is of little interest? As the end-user of a system, you are bound by the interfaces of the system in question. The interfaces of a system determine your productivity. Its interfaces define the productivity of a business. This is a metric that is not understood with enough depth as companies increasingly introduce newer IT functionality. Generally, increased function means increased interactions unless the new part is hidden away from the end-user in what we can call *the back office*. Alas, it often appears in *the front office* where the customers and clients roam.

Figure 123 Why am I doing this? This is icing on the cake!

The right experts for the job

In manufacturing processes, you have experts in production methods, Production Engineers, making the process efficient and *lean and mean.* In IT system developments, you have experts, Programme and Project Managers, who understand the development process and ensure that the best balance of emphasis is used and achieved. Any development project is a trade-off of function delivered, time, resources, costs, and quality. This is where the IT equivalent of manufacturing *lean and mean* is to be found. The focus is on how the system is developed and deployed, not how the end-users efficiently use it when deployed.

Figure 124 Cut out the excesses

Figure 125 The only secure system is a stopped one!

Increasingly today, there is a need for a system's security to be fit-for-purpose, at a minimum. There has to be confidence in security. Data, especially personal data, must be fully protected. The system must be protected from hackers, either deliberate hackers or chance hackers, who can render the system inoperable or make its behaviour fraudulent. Security experts look at the whole life-cycle of the system's development from business inception to deployment and beyond into continued operations. But sometimes they overegg the pudding. The following is a real-life experience.

The password puzzle

The author was once working in a group of experts, and some critical design specification about a new product was stolen and ended up with the competition. The management of the whole project suddenly sprung into action and reviewed security. They issued the instruction that passwords were to be changed once per month.

Figure 126 Open sesame

Hearing this in a meeting, a collogue next to me said; my dog isn't going to enjoy having his name changed every month. The data had not been stolen because of a weak password or a cracked password. It had been stolen by what we can call physical means. The management missed the real point of the need for change. They had acted outside that need and created an instance of bureaucracy. The bureaucracy means that users have to change and remember new passwords, and the bureaucracy of someone having to check that they, the end-users, had changed their passwords once per month. Secure passwords are a proper discipline but making changes when they are not needed is bureaucracy.

Passwords are a particular sandpit in which bureaucrats can play and cause significant frustration on innocent end-users. Passwords are an essential part of the privacy of a user's data and digital services. They unlock these for the genuine user and block any malicious or accidental users. But how often do we encounter one of the following password frustrations?

- Wrong password! I've forgotten my password! I did write it down, but I've forgotten where. Recover password! I've forgotten how to recover my password! I'm sorry I cannot tell you your password over the phone!
- Password must be changed. You have used that password before – thereby showing that they are keeping your old passwords. Where? Why? For how long?
- Password must contain at least 8 characters, 2 numbers, and 1 special character (aren't all characters special?). So now the password isn't a word; it is a combination of symbols. It becomes hard to remember now.
- Password must not contain words. This instruction means that the password is a special jumble and especially hard to remember. Some password generators will provide such jumbles.
- Advice is to have a different password for each login. This, along with the jumbles, means that no one can remember their passwords. The answer

to this dilemma is to have a password manager that logs and keeps them for you.

- How do you get into a password manager? Use a single password.

Yes, there are other ways of entering a system like fingerprint and face recognition, but systems enabled with these functions sometimes ask for a password, or passcode, or something that has to be remembered.

The whole passwords environment is obstructive, not just for those who need to be obstructed but for those who don't need to be.

There is a need for such a cadre of *expert professionals* to meet Obstructive Bureaucrats' challenge in this Information Age. Experts whose sole purpose is to ensure that the end-user interfaces are free from Obstructive Bureaucracy's hindrances. These experts are, by inference, minimalists.

Key messages from this chapter

The Essential Design of an IT system is the foundation design which means that the system works doing the required job and no more. In this context, any more is bureaucracy and has been designed-in to satisfy the apparent needs of bureaucrats with the direct or indirect intent of slowing things down.

Think and imagine that you are designing and specifying an IT system:

- The end-users' efficiency is essential[55], and this is like ordering a pizza. You are not ordering two or three or four pizzas; you are ordering one.
- You are walking at 4 miles per hour and are 4 miles away from a stout brick wall. You cannot stop for precisely 1 hour less than 0.1 seconds. Do not exceed the 4 miles per hour speed unless you want an abrupt halt.
- You have $3, dollars no more, to buy ice cream. Order the £3 ice cream, not the $4 one and don't expect change.
- Think within the box for once, not outside it.

---

[55] Many will argue that this applies to all end-user IT systems that have ever been designed or will ever be designed. Make your own mind up about this.

26. Cultural change

Abstract

This chapter, which is the final and concluding chapter of this book, considers the enormous challenge, the Grand Challenge that **Obstructive Bureaucracy** throws over our progress in these present times. We put forward some very radical proposals to deal with the negativity of **Obstructive Bureaucracy** in this Information Age.

Our goal is to increase the size of this:

Figure 127 The national treasure

And to dump Obstructive Bureaucracy and **Clutteridge** to this receptacle.

Figure 128 Bureaucracy is rubbish.

Setting the scene

After the ramblings and rantings of this book, the time has come to propose what might be a solution, be it partial, to the challenge that has been articulated. First, though, it is appropriate to stand-back and state where we see the challenge we have called **Obstructive Bureaucracy**.

1. Bureaucracy, obstructive or not, has been around since the dawn of human intelligence.
2. Over time its effects and form have changed as technology has advanced with human progress.
3. The second half of the 20th Century saw the microchip's advancement and digital IT's ubiquitous use. Affordability and useability were available and capable by *the many*.
4. This use has been both positive in driving progress and negative in enabling bureaucracy.

5. Unless the hostile forces of **Obstructive Bureaucracy** are minimised, any nation's growth and progress will flounder.
6. There needs to be a significant fundamental change in the ways that we chip away at **Obstructive Bureaucracy**.

The possible changes needed

The possible changes needed have got to be significant and radical simply because the challenge is immense and threatening. The following could be tried;

1. Someone could write a book defining and highlighting the adverse effects of **Obstructive Bureaucracy** and introducing such terms a **Clutteridge** and even describing who are the purveyors of the dark art. You, as the reader, decide whether this goal can or has been met.[56]
2. Educational institutions could insert the elements of anti-bureaucratic design considerations into their course syllabuses. Industry could champion the cause, especially the IT industry itself.
3. A government might sponsor a website that educates about the practice of **Obstructive Bureaucracy** and proposes counter actions.
4. Businesses and governments might create a major executive post that is missioned to stamp-out **Obstructive Bureaucracy**.

The above are all positive activities that will reduce **Obstructive Bureaucracy**, but they are probably not enough. So what radical and fundamental change is needed?

Radical change

We started this book by stating that an advanced industrial nation like the UK has a meagre economic growth rate, and therefore, its wealth as a nation is not progressing as quickly as many feel that it should. This proposition heavily implies an economic view of the changes needed has to be adopted. There is little chance that a consistent picture of a country's national economic structure like the UK can be agreed upon by all. So, let us propose one. You can make up your own, but for now, the picture below is far from complete and is only fit for our narrow views as bureaucratic fighters. It is overly simplistic, but what a joy that is rather than it being too complicated.

---

[56] The author of this book supports this.

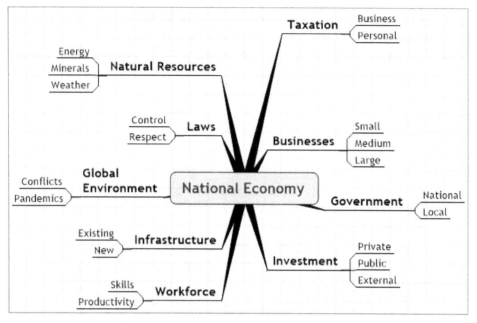

Figure 129 The national economy

Now go round the various labels in the figure above, or your preferred tags, and see where you believe **Obstructive Bureaucracy** lurks and prevents real progress.

You will probably come out with a figure like the next one where those labels in **BOLD** are its habitat. The colour red has been chosen because of its deep psychological connection with red-tape, which we discussed earlier.

We might postulate that the new picture looks like this:

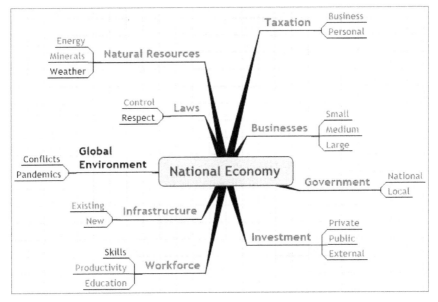

Figure 130 The National Economy again

You can choose your preferred red labels, but it is most probable that you will see a scenario as above where **Obstructive Bureaucracy** is pervasive. It's everywhere. We can further conclude that what we are facing is even more significant and more pervasive than we thought. The solution has to be so!

What is needed is a real national leader who will realise that this is a significant national problem and takes actions to eradicate it. Not a leader who nods and agrees (doesn't everyone?) that it is a problem and pigeon holes it for a study sometime. Yes, we must ensure that bureaucracy doesn't hinder us – Next item. A leader who will see

Figure 131 The ups and downs

that there is a problem of meagre growth in the UK and across most of Europe that we fail to unlock the IT age's potential. We are failing not because we are not using and applying IT but because we are using it far too much for the negative force of **Obstructive Bureaucracy**. The efficiencies of IT are being neutralised. Action and Reaction are, on too many occasions, opposite.

We have now introduced the word *efficiencies,* and perhaps this is where part of the answer lies. We could have a focused government department, The Department of Efficiency. Opening our opinions to temptation, we might call it The Department of Anti **Obstructive Bureaucracy**, but this is a clumsy negative term. It's also long-winded, perhaps even bureaucratic. The Department of Efficiency is a much more positive title. Its mission would be to enable the use of IT and to monitor and stamp-out **Obstructive Bureaucracy**. Its reach would be across all aspects of national life, not just what we call *industry*. It would mainly look for governmental bureaucracy because of the numbers of people affected by national systems.

It could then sponsor an institute perhaps named The Institute of National Efficiency, which could bring together some of the nation's experts on how you avoid unnecessary roadblocks to growth in traditional industries and across the whole of national activity. In turn, this institute could define and sponsor educational courses to enable efficiency and disabling **Obstructive Bureaucracy**. This institute would not be an institute focused on engineering or an institute focused on IT, or an institute focused on economics. These exist and have cultures of their own.

Figure 132 Banned

The education would focus on what we called in a previous chapter; Essential Design. It is no more and no less than the design needed to achieve the necessary actions that an IT interface must do to meet its goal. The inputs and outputs' design and the time an end-user has to spend at the interface to execute a specific and essential task, not to display her or his elite IT skills.

The summation of the change

What is needed is a radical change in the way that we deal with our modern national economy. IT has done and will continue to spread itself across what we can call the old industry sectors and professions in a fair and wrong way. IT

Figure 133 Learn from me

is, of course, an industry sector, but it is everywhere in all of the other industries and the private lives of individuals. Perhaps the nearest analogy that we can make to it is what happened when the power of steam proliferated. It didn't only increase in the Victorian world's factories and workshops but also enabled rail travel and opened up the whole realm. It enabled sea travel and opened up the world as a whole, especially The New World. Steam helped the heating of buildings and homes. Steam enabled water to be supplied to cities and towns. It allowed giant warships to be commissioned. Steam affected everyone everywhere. It was a revolution and powered evolution. IT is doing the same, but the benefits are often masked by what we keep calling **Obstructive Bureaucracy**.

So what have we proposed to deal with the uncovering of the real growth potential that IT can bring us:

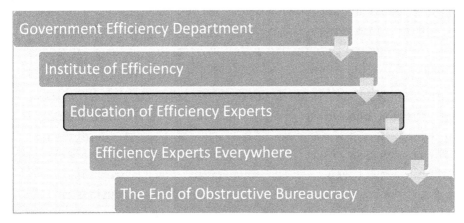

Figure 134 The Efficiency Fous

Just perhaps being radical, we might turn the solution on its head and think out of the box, or at least think from another side of the box. Rather than climbing up the Efficiency Hilltop and trumpeting the solution from it, we might make a direct assault on the Bureaucracy Hilltop and trumpet from there with a clear anti-bureaucracy mission. In which case, our scheme as above becomes:

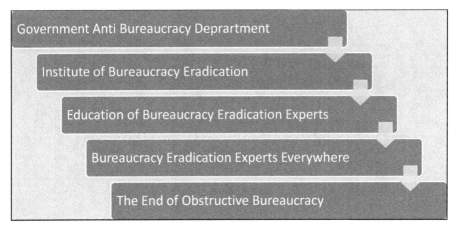

Figure 135 The Eradication Focus

The Long Conclusion from this chapter and of this book

The conclusion that we now reach is a long one in terms of text and time to read it. This is because, like so many difficult challenges, there isn't an easy answer. The suggestions given are mainly proposals of what the answer may look like and contain.

We know that there is a need for some new and focused approach in a changing world because of IT's advances and IT application. Application for the good of **Progress** and the bad **Obstructive Bureaucracy**. Many will not accept this, and the non-acceptance is, in itself, a problem. We can name them bureaucrats, modern Luddites and yesterday's people who are, as this book has explained, nothing new but the descendants of a long line of *their type*.

We need a new national focus, or hopefully a global focus on how we stamp out **Obstructive Bureaucracy** and how we light a bonfire of the **Clutteridge** that characterises it. The change will be a significant one starting at the top and percolating everywhere, just as IT has oozed everywhere. Somehow, we need a new way of seeing what is happening and why it is happening. Just trying to make business, commerce, society, and personal activities more efficient isn't a sufficient and broad enough answer. We need to ensure that they have efficiency designed-in rather than tuned-in. Pictorially we have:

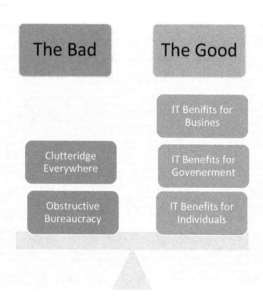

Figure 136 New approach and balance needed.

There needs to be a new way of designing user interfaces to minimise user time and patience levels. Just letting business and techies specify and create them is opening them up to retrograde bureaucratic overload. In turn, this overload is what we said was the challenge at the start of this book. We must not continue with the current ways as these are leading us further into the bureaucratic quagmire.

Figure 137
It's BIG

Overall, we can conclude that we live in civilised but challenging times. Humans have progressed through many stages; many of these steps have involved disseminating information about essential change matters. How these changes are delivered has progressed. But in the last, say, 30 years, the changes have accelerated at a staggering rate. This rate is fuelled by the advances in chip power and affordability. Data is everywhere; information surrounds us, sometimes swamps us. IT devices and systems are everywhere, and it seems that everything connects to everything. The business of many nations in all its forms is embracing IT and pushing forward. But there is a headwind, and It is called **Obstructive Bureaucracy.** It must be moderated or deflected if we are to manage to grow at more than a meagre rate as in the immediate past.

We need to tackle the growth of **Obstructive Bureaucracy** in all its guises, and we need a change led from the top to do that. We need a whole new and radically different focus on efficiency, covering every part of our lives for business activities and personal activities. We need this new focus to be organised and sponsored. If we don't get it soon, we'll drown in an ocean of **Obstructive Bureaucracy.**

Figure 138 Ups and Downs

Before we go back down the progress hill. The effort must be institutionalised, but in this, there is a danger of creating more bureaucracy. With our current practices and mindsets, we might agree that there is a vital challenge. We might agree that it must be tackled. But then we'll set up a classic bureaucratic establishment or institution to take up the challenge, and it will pontificate for years on end, holding meetings and documenting its lack of progress with bureaucratic lagging.

Yes, there is a distinct risk that this institution will be a bureaucracy itself. Oh, dear!

> **Father to son; They are picking the England Cricket Team today.**
>
> **Son; Who?**
>
> **Father; The England Cricket Selectors**
>
> **Son; Who picks the England Cricket Selectors?**
>
> **Father; Stop asking so many questions.**

How can we think out-of-the-box without encountering the bureaucrats in the box? Who are the thinkers who can plot the escape? What's the landscape that we are probably looking at here? We know it's not simple. It's multi-faceted, deep-seated in business and personal life. The solution is therefore likewise, but we can begin to say where parts of the solution The Bureaucratic Challenge might lie:

Seek, and ye shall find

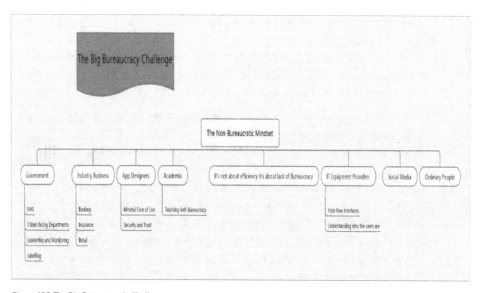

Figure 139 The Big Bureaucratic Challenge

The Bureaucratic Challenge Big Tickets

Above, you can see a suggested breakdown of how the Non-Bureaucratic Mindset might see the challenge. As explored below for what might be the beginnings of a solution to the bureaucratic waste that we have identified in this book, it is a framework. It is by no means complete. It is a start.

The Non-Bureaucratic Mindset Framework
- **Government**: Needs to embrace the Non-Bureaucratic Mindset as a national challenge and understand its contribution to national growth and progress.
    - o NHS: This is the National Health Service of the UK, but in many countries, remote-digital medicine is part of the future and making it as bureaucracy free as possible is essential since this is a new channel.
    - o Citizen facing Departments: Because governments serve the citizens, the citizen-facing interfaces must be bureaucracy free.

- o Leadership and Monitoring: Only governments can lead the national effort in terms of direct leadership and finance. But there needs to be supervision, especially the monitoring of effectiveness.
- o Labelling: It may be possible to grade and label service applications and the infrastructure that they execute on to show the end-user the expected difficulty and complexity of the interface, say high, medium, low.
- **Industry Business**: There is an obvious need for businesses to provide their digital services to as many end-users as possible. It implies that they design upwards from the lowest skilled and capable end-users. It is in the interest of most businesses to do this.
  - o Banking: The introduction of digital banking, especially the use of digital payments replacing cash transactions, means that banks must make their Internet Banking Systems as simple as the least-informed user. Banks, through credit card transactions, are often the final stage of a retail transaction. Banks must make their system 'trusted' by the end-users are not open to stray questions that can undermine trust.
  - o Insurance: The insurance industry for personal, auto or property insurance is increasingly online-only, and this means that the interface to the customer systems must be as terse and easy to understand. Long contracts are not easy to read on small smartphone screens. So the longer the contracts are padded-out with bureaucratic excess, the harder they are to read. Does one wonder if anyone does read an insurance contract? Perhaps this is what the bureaucrats intend?
  - o Retail: when you go into a physical retail outlet, you may browse if you don't know what you want. Generally, you are not hosed-down before, during or after your visit. Why do many retail interfaces stream unwanted information at the end-user, most of which is additional to the act of purchasing?
- **App Designers**: They hold the key to how the app interfaces with the end-users, so if they are not tight on the
  - o Minimal Ease of Use
  - o Security and Trust
- **An App**: This is something somewhat left-field and hopeful. This book has been written with the assistance of a Grammar Checker, which is itself an application. The writer needs this because if you think this book's grammar is 'low', you should have seen it before the Grammar

Checker got to work on it. Perhaps someone could design and deliver a Bureaucracy Checker?

- o This new app informs the developer, and hopefully, the end-user of an app and service that bureaucracy was 'around' and wasting time. Current Grammar Checkers identify excessive words and phrases, so extensions into bureaucracy as we have identified it should not be possible.
- o The app could identify:
  - Extra input and output verbiage at the end-user interface, especially screens.
  - Extra information that is not pertinent to the prime purpose of the service being used.
  - Extra time being spent by the end-user up and above what the designers see as minimal.
  - Perhaps the app could grade the service for bureaucracy and time-wasting.

The app could even use AI to make itself more and more bureaucracy aware and sensitive. The app could be labelled with the word Smart to give the feeling of being helpful, hopefully.

- **Academia**: There needs to be something like a new branch of economics that focuses explicitly on bureaucracy's effects on growth, wealth, and progress.
  - o Teaching Anti-Bureaucracy
  - o Methods to measure the effects of bureaucracy.
- **IT Equipment Providers**: They must provide digital platforms that do not encourage bureaucracy and extra processes that intensionally or unintentionally inhibit progress. Many service apps assume that end-users have good digital skills to use them. This is a big assumption since a large proportion of the population does not have such skills.
  - o Hide Raw Interfaces of hardware and operating systems
  - o Understanding who the users are.
- **Social Media**: Too much information extracted from input data behind the back of the end-user. The result is too much-unsolicited information filling up inboxes and taking time to look-at and delete.
- **Ordinary People**: A realisation and recognition everywhere that ordinary people do not like bureaucracy. It gets in the way of their lifestyle activities by consuming their free time. It consumes their work time. It consumes them.

Final Conclusion

Bureaucracy consumes everything that it touches, and in these digital days, it touches everywhere, everything and everyone[57].

Figure 140 Don't let bureaucracy go to or over your head

---

[57] A final conclusion longer than this would have been bureaucratic!!!!!

27.   Appendices

Appendix A

Make more Bs to make more As

Since Victorian times in public houses (pubs) in the UK, beer had been drawn from the barrels by what we called beer pumps or beer engines. These pumps were and still are, arranged in rows on the bar counters. They worked through pressure being lowered by a cylinder's action; the beer would flow even upwards from the barrels, probably below in a cellar. They are beautiful examples of practical engineering

In the 1960s, a revolution happened in the provision of beers. Brewers produced a new kind of beer that they decanted into steel kegs. These kegs were connected to gas systems in the pubs, and the liquid was blown into the waiting glass. The old beer pumps were replaced

Figure 141
Bottoms up! and trashed, being obsolete now the new keg age had dawned. But the quality of the beer was a retrograde step from the old ale of yesteryear. Serious beer drinkers demanded a foamy head and, above all, flavour in-depth. Traditions die hard amongst serious beer drinkers in the UK and, say, Denmark and Germany.

So the old ways were demanded by customers, and the brewers had to make an about-turn. Alas, all the beer pumps of the old-style had been trashed. Worse than that, these beer pumps were works of precision engineering, and suddenly it was realised that there was only one craftsman left who could produce them. His production was limited to a few per week. The outlook for the brewers and the beer drinkers was bleak. But then, some bright spark, the UK has them in abundance, proposed that the single craftsman stopped making the pumps. Consternation was rife. Instead, he should tutor several apprentices in the art of making the pumps and then after a month or so, and the production problem would be solved. It was solved.

The solution worked and is testimony to thinking about how to be more productive.

Appendix B

The Romans

This subject is something of a sidetrack from the main themes, but it is an interesting observation of information and how it might just change.

The Romans, or the Age of Rome, was from 27 BC to 1453. At its peak, the Roman empire was well over 4 million square kilometres. The Romans were one of the pivotal forms of the Western World's civilisations, for good or bad depending on your views. As far as we know, their military might was backed by a considerable bureaucracy. Some of which executed their essential governance, some of which were undoubtedly like the Obstructive Bureaucracy we have today.

In many countries, the mention of Roman and Rome's words start a debate about the legacies of the Roman way of life. Some people might even burst into Latin to sing the praises of that way of life. The Romans were generally revered and associated with the progress of humankind. In 1979, the Monty Python film *The Life of Brian* featured a scene in a dark room with the cast suitably clad in dark robes. It's a meeting, and the chairman of the meeting says: *What have the Romans ever done for us?* The following suggestions are then uttered; *aqueduct, sanitation, roads, irrigation, medicine, education, wine, public baths, safety in the streets, peace.*

From that moment when the film was seen, especially today at any time and place in the UK and probably in many other countries, at the mention of the word Roman, someone will utter; *What have the Romans ever done for us?* And those close will begin to recite the list as above. We had, and still have, a lot of information about the Roman civilisation, which lasted us as information for some 15 centuries, but it was all suddenly superseded by the dialogue of that scene! It wasn't proved to be wrong; it was superseded. Sometimes the information world that we live in changes in a strange way and direction.

Appendix C

The Owl and the Pussy-Cat

This poem was written by Edward Lear in 1871 and published in his book Nonsense Songs, Stories, Botany and Alphabets. It was written for a three-year-old girl, but no matter what you are age is, it fascinates one's mind and asks the question; *is it nonsense or not?*[58]

---

[58] For those who have ploughed through this book you will have read that the text was 'toned and edited' by a Grammar Checker. The Grammar Checker used was not happy with Lear's grammar in this poem but the author was stringently kept the Grammar Checker from performing changes. These would indeed have been nonsensical, perhaps even bureaucractic.

I
The Owl and the Pussy-cat went to sea
  In a beautiful pea-green boat,
They took some honey, and plenty of money,
  Wrapped up in a five-pound note.
The Owl looked up to the stars above,
  And sang to a small guitar,
"O lovely Pussy! O Pussy, my love,
  What a beautiful Pussy you are,
     You are,
     You are!
What a beautiful Pussy you are!"

II
Pussy said to the Owl, "You elegant fowl!
  How charmingly sweet you sing!
O let us be married! too long we have tarried:
  But what shall we do for a ring?"
They sailed away, for a year and a day,
  To the land where the Bong-Tree grows
And there in a wood a Piggy-wig stood
  With a ring at the end of his nose,
    His nose,
    His nose,
  With a ring at the end of his nose.

III
"Dear Pig, are you willing to sell for one shilling
  Your ring?" Said the Piggy, "I will."
So they took it away, and were married next day
  By the Turkey who lives on the hill.

They dined on mince, and slices of quince,
  Which they ate with a runcible spoon;
And hand in hand, on the edge of the sand,
  They danced by the light of the moon,
      The moon,
      The moon,
They danced by the light of the moon.

Source: *The Random House Book of Poetry for Children* (1983)

And The Owl and the Pussy-Cat by Edward Lear | Poetry Foundation

28. References Bibliography

BBC. *Age of Outrage.* 17 February 2020.
https://www.bbc.co.uk/programmes/p083mv25.

Economics, Trading. "United Kingdom GDP Growth Rate."
https://tradingeconomics.com/. 2020.
https://tradingeconomics.com/united-kingdom/gdp-growth.

Francis Chittenden, Hilary Foster, Brian Sloan. "Taxation and Red Tape."
https://iea.org.uk. 17 February 2010.
https://iea.org.uk/publications/research/taxation-and-red-tape-the-
cost-to-british-business-of-complying-with-the-uk-ta.

King, John Kay and Mervyn. *Radical Uncertainty.* The Bridge Street Press, 2020.

2001 A Space Odyssey. Directed by Stanley Kubrick. 1968.

Nabil Abu el Ata, Maurice J Perks. *Solving the Dynamic Complexity Dilemma.*
Springer, 2014.

Smith, Adam. *The Wealth of Nations.* William Strahan, Thomas Cadell, 1776.

The Monty Python film The Meaning of Life. 1983.

Whitney, John. *Unintended Consequences.* 2010.

29.   List of Figures

Index

Index

End of book, Book end, Bookend, End[59]

---

[59] Beaurocracy to end with.